PENGUIN BOOKS

101 THINGS YOU THOUGHT YOU
KNEW ABOUT THE *TITANIC*...
BUT DIDN'T!

Tim Maltin is a London businessman who has been researching the *Titanic* in his spare time for the last twenty-five years. Captivated by the sinking since he was only seven years old and first saw the film version of Walter Lord's *A Night To Remember*, Tim has made a detailed study of the public enquiries into the disaster and the extraordinary atmospheric conditions that night. Tim is a marketing and PR consultant and lives in the Wiltshire countryside with his wife and two children.

PENGUIN BOOKS

Published by the Penguin Group
Penguin Group (USA) Inc., 375 Hudson Street, New York, New York 10014, U.S.A.
Penguin Group (Canada), 90 Eglinton Avenue East, Suite 700, Toronto,
Ontario, Canada M4P 2Y3 (a division of Pearson Penguin Canada Inc.)
Penguin Books Ltd, 80 Strand, London WC2R 0RL, England
Penguin Ireland, 25 St Stephen's Green, Dublin 2, Ireland (a division of Penguin Books Ltd)
Penguin Group (Australia), 250 Camberwell Road, Camberwell,
Victoria 3124, Australia (a division of Pearson Australia Group Pty Ltd)
Penguin Books India Pvt Ltd, 11 Community Centre,
Panchsheel Park, New Delhi – 110 017, India
Penguin Group (NZ), 67 Apollo Drive, Rosedale, Auckland 0632,
New Zealand (a division of Pearson New Zealand Ltd)
Penguin Books (South Africa) (Pty) Ltd, 24 Sturdee Avenue,
Rosebank, Johannesburg 2196, South Africa

Penguin Books Ltd, Registered Offices:
80 Strand, London WC2R 0RL, England

First published in Great Britain by Beautiful Books Limited 2010
First published in the United States of America by Penguin Books,
a member of Penguin Group (USA) Inc. 2011

1 3 5 7 9 10 8 6 4 2

Copyright © Tim Maltin and Eloise Aston, 2010
All rights reserved

ISBN 978-0-14-311909-8
CIP data available

Printed in the United States of America

Contents

Maiden Voyage

Passengers

'Iceberg, right ahead!'

Collision

SOS

The Californian Incident

Women and Children First

Final Moments

Aftermath

101 Things You Thought
You Knew About
the *Titanic* . . .
but Didn't!

Preface

Jack Thayer was only seventeen years old when he survived the sinking of the *Titanic* by swimming to an overturned lifeboat. His father died in the disaster and his rude awakening into adulthood no doubt coloured his perspective; but in his privately published 1940 account of the sinking, this is how Jack recalled what life was like before the *Titanic* sank:

> 'There was peace and the world had an even tenor to its way. Nothing was revealed in the morning the trend of which was not known the night before. It seems to me that the disaster about to occur was the event that not only made the world rub its eyes and awake but woke it with a start keeping it moving at a rapidly accelerating pace ever since with less and less peace, satisfaction and happiness. To my mind the world of today awoke April 15th, 1912.'

The sinking of the *Titanic* on April 15th, 1912 was as shocking to the world as the destruction of the Twin Towers on September 11th, 2001. *Titanic* triggered the first global media storm, with *The New York Times* devoting its first twelve pages to the story: the newest, largest and most luxurious ship in the world, the unsinkable *Titanic*, packed with many of the biggest celebrities of the day, had sunk on her maiden voyage, with catastrophic loss of life.

As soon as her survivors disembarked in New York from the rescue ship *Carpathia* and told their stories, the world began a game of Chinese Whispers about what really happened the night the *Titanic* sank. Each survivor only saw a small piece of the complete picture of what happened and the press in 1912 attempted to fill in the gaps as sensationally as possible. As a result, wild rumours developed, many of which still persist today.

The *Titanic* disaster was the subject of contemporary public inquiries on both sides of the Atlantic and is consequently one of the best-documented disasters in history. These Hearings corrected many of the rumours circulating at the time, but they also propagated new ones of their own. As *Titanic* passes into folklore, old myths persist and new ones continue to be created to suit the worldview of new generations—and cinema audiences. The result is that what most people know about *Titanic* today is a mixture of fact and fiction.

As Lord Byron said in his comic-epic poem, *Don Juan*, in 1823:

'T is strange,—but true; for truth is always strange;
Stranger than fiction; if it could be told,
How much would novels gain by the exchange!
How differently the world would men behold!

This was never truer than in the case of *Titanic*. The difficulty however—as Byron points out—is how to tell it. I hope that the accessible format of this book will be a way in, for some, to discovering the truth about the *Titanic*. Where possible, I have tried to get at this through eye witness testimony, which is fully quoted and referenced.

As Walter Lord observed in both his classic 1957 account of the sinking, *A Night To Remember* and his 1986 sequel, *The Night Lives On*:

> 'It is a rash man indeed who would set himself up as final arbiter on all that happened the incredible night the *Titanic* went down.'

This book is not intended as the final word on any of the 101 points it covers, but it is intended to make you think differently about the *Titanic*.

Tim Maltin, 15th April 2010

Notes on the text

The US Inquiry, which began on 19th April, 1912 and finished on 25th May, 1912, numbered its questions by witness. For example, CHL100 is the 100th question asked to Charles Herbert Lightoller, *Titanic*'s most senior surviving Officer.

The British Inquiry, which began on 2nd May, 1912 and finished on 3rd July, 1912, numbered its questions in simple chronological order, regardless of witness initials. For example, question number 16802 happens to be the first question asked to Charles Herbert Lightoller on the 14th day of that inquiry.

In May 1915 Limitation of Liability Hearings regarding the *Titanic* were held in the US, but these do not have numbered questions as the testimony itself has been lost, with only some witness depositions presently available.

Wherever this book quotes from the US or British Inquiries, I have included the official question number, so the reader may easily conduct his own research at www. titanicinquiry.org.

Details of the author's forthcoming book *A Very Deceiving Night*, together with articles and other *Titanic* information and links, can be found at www.averydeceivingnight.com, where I also welcome your comments and questions on this book.

The Ship

I TITANIC WAS THE LARGEST SHIP IN THE WORLD IN 1912.

Yes, but only just. *Titanic* was built to the same design as her slightly older twin sister, *Olympic*, launched about seven months before Titanic on 20th October, 1910. *Olympic*, *Titanic* and *Britannic*, the third sister of the *Olympic* Class trio, were all 882ft 9ins long. *Titanic* and her older sister *Olympic* were almost identical, the only visual difference being *Olympic*'s open A Deck promenade, which was later enclosed on *Titanic* and *Britannic*. However, *Titanic* also differed from *Olympic* in other small respects, including extended B Deck Staterooms and additional cabins, giving her a Gross Register Tonnage (GRT) of 46,328, only 1,204 GRT (or 2%) larger than *Olympic* at 45,124 GRT, but nonetheless just enough to give *Titanic* the title of largest liner in the world. However, *Olympic*, as the first in this new class of superliner, was 42% larger than the previous largest ship in the world, Cunard's *Mauretania*, at only 31,738 GRT.

For this reason, *Olympic*'s building and launch attracted much more public interest than *Titanic*'s.

Olympic was later to learn from the disaster which occurred to her younger sister, as after the *Titanic* sank, *Olympic* was withdrawn from service in order to increase her watertight protection and lifeboat provision. These modifications were also built into the *Britannic*, which then became a slightly larger ship again at 48,158 GRT. *Olympic* outlived both her younger sisters, travelling at least 1.8 million miles during her eventful career and continuing in successful service until she was scrapped in 1935 following American restrictions on the emigrant trade and an increase in the popularity of travelling across the Atlantic by airplane.

2 TITANIC WAS THE FASTEST SHIP IN THE WORLD IN 1912.

No, the *Mauretania* and the *Lusitania*, built by Cunard in 1906, were both significantly faster than the *Olympic* and *Titanic*, whose owners, the White Star Line, had not tried to compete on speed since the *Oceanic II* was launched on January 14th, 1899. She and all subsequent White Star vessels were built for size and luxury, rather than speed. The *Mauretania* had a guaranteed service speed of no less than 24 knots, with a maximum recorded speed of 28 knots, and had since 1909 held the Blue Riband for the fastest westbound Atlantic crossing, a record which lasted for two decades. She had also broken the eastbound speed record in 1907, but only the westbound leg was counted for the Blue Riband. The *Lusitania* was slightly slower, but still had a guaranteed service speed of 24 knots, compared with the *Olympic*-class's designed service speed of 21.5 knots.

The *Olympic*-class ships were designed to be larger than their rivals to attract the emigrant trade, and also to attract the more wealthy with the comfort of the first and second class accommodation. White Star Line was able to offer a smoother passage for all classes, without the vibration that the Cunarders' quadruple screws gave at high speeds, achieving at the same time a significant economy of running costs, as fuel consumption was correspondingly lower. *Olympic* consumed about 650 tons of coal per twenty four hours with an average speed of 21.7 knots on her maiden voyage, compared to 1000 tons of coal per twenty four hours for both the *Lusitania* and *Mauretania*. Although they would not have noticed the saving in fuel, passengers did notice and appreciate how smooth *Olympic* and *Titanic* were.

3 TITANIC WAS GENUINELY BELIEVED TO BE UNSINKABLE.

Yes. As White Star Chairman and *Titanic* survivor Joseph Bruce Ismay confirmed at the British enquiry:

> 18755: 'I think the position was taken up that the ship was looked upon as practically unsinkable; she was looked upon as being a lifeboat in herself.'

This belief stemmed from *Titanic* being designed to float with any two of her watertight compartments flooded, or all of her forward three, as no-one could imagine anything worse than a breach of two compartments through a collision on a bulkhead, as happened in the *Olympic/Hawke* collision. The fact that no-one anticipated the glancing blow such as *Titanic* received from the iceberg, a blow which damaged the hull along a 300ft area and breached six watertight compartments, is not surprising, as this type of side-swipe disaster had never occurred before in recorded maritime history.

This design feature led not only the White Star Line but also the well-respected trade journal *The Shipbuilder* to call *Titanic* 'practically unsinkable', a term also used to describe other large liners with watertight subdivisions, including Cunard's Mauretania. In this extract from The Shipbuilder, the marvels of the Olympic-class's watertight doors are extolled:

> '...so that in the event of accident, or at any time when it may be considered advisable, the captain can, by simply moving an electric switch, instantly close the doors throughout and make the vessel practically unsinkable.'

It is often said that no-one seriously believed the *Titanic* was unsinkable, and that the press created this myth in the aftermath of the disaster to highlight the 'hubris' of such reliance on man-made technology, but they really did believe that she was 'practically unsinkable'. For example, *Titanic* survivor Elmer Taylor, heard Captain Smith explaining on *Titanic's* maiden voyage that the ship could be 'cut crosswise into three pieces and each piece would float', a remark which confirmed Taylor's belief in the safety of the ship. Captain Smith probably got this information from Thomas Andrews, Managing Director of *Titanic's* builders. Andrews was travelling on *Titanic* on her maiden voyage and, as was reported on April 29th, 1912:

> 'Mrs. Eleanor Cassebeer declared this afternoon that
> Thomas Andrews of the firm of Harlan and Wolf [sic],
> builders of the ship, sat next to her at the table and
> frequently told her that the steamer had been started
> before it was finished, but that even though it should
> be cut into three pieces it would still float.'

Thomas Andrews was correct, but instead of the iceberg
safely cutting *Titanic* into three pieces, it punctured all of
her first six watertight compartments. Such freak damage
was not considered a 'practical' possibility before the *Titanic*
disaster.

Captain Smith's belief in the safety of modern shipbuilding
was recalled in the aftermath of the disaster by the *New York
Times*, on April 16th, 1912, when they quoted the following
interview which Captain Smith had given in 1907, after his
successful completion of the maiden voyage of the Adriatic:

> 'Capt. Smith maintained that shipbuilding was such a
> perfect art nowadays that absolute disaster, involving
> the passengers on a great modern liner, was quite
> unthinkable. Whatever happened, he contended, there
> would be time before the vessel sank to save the lives
> of every person on board. "I will go a bit further," he
> said. "I will say that I cannot imagine any condition
> which could cause a ship to founder. I cannot conceive
> of any vital disaster happening to this vessel. Modern
> shipbuilding has gone beyond that."'

It is similarly telling that, when James Bisset, Second Officer of the rescue ship *Carpathia*, visited the *Olympic* after her maiden voyage in New York, a year before the *Titanic* sank, her officers informed him that she was unsinkable.

As reports of the disaster began to come in on 15th April, 1912, Philip Franklin, Vice-President of the White Star Line told the public:

> 'We place absolute confidence in the *Titanic*. We believe that the boat is unsinkable.'

Titanic's passengers thought the same and, even when the ship was sinking, many were reluctant to get into her lifeboats because they couldn't believe that she would really sink and that a lifeboat would be safer.

In Walter Lord's famous account, *A Night to Remember*, he tells the story of Louis Ogden, a passenger on the rescue ship *Carpathia*. On inquiring about the reasons for the crew's sudden activity, he was told that the *Titanic* was sinking and that he was to stay in his cabin. Nonetheless, he got his family up and told them to put on their warmest clothes and get ready to evacuate. He couldn't believe that the *Titanic* was sinking, concluding it was more likely that his own ship was on fire! It took what happened to the *Titanic*, one of the worst maritime disasters in peacetime, to convince people that no ship could ever be truly unsinkable.

4 TITANIC WAS ORIGINALLY TO HAVE BEEN NAMED GIGANTIC.

No, but her younger sister, *Britannic*, may have been initially intended to have that name. Press speculation about a White Star liner with the name *Gigantic* extended as far back as the late 19th Century and the name continued to crop up from time to time, even as late as 1913, but there is no hard evidence that the name *Gigantic* was ever officially used.

It has often been suggested that the *Britannic*, the third sister in the *Olympic* class, was originally intended to be named *Gigantic* but that this name was changed following the *Titanic* disaster; and White Star's knowledge of the forthcoming new large German liners such as the *Imperator*, which would take the title of world's largest liner from *Olympic* a few months after the *Titanic* sank. Indeed, several newspaper reports, the trade journal *The Engineer* and Yard No. 433's anchor supplier, all refer to the third ship in the Olympic Class as *Gigantic*. However, Harland and Wolff's own order book refers to Yard No. 433 only, although the name *Britannic* has been written in next to it, for which they had received a formal order to proceed on 28th June, 1911. Although the date that the name *Britannic* was entered into the order book is difficult to prove, its existence next to the June 1911 entry tends to indicate that, if the third sister was ever to have been named *Gigantic*, then this idea was abandoned in favour of *Britannic* long before the *Titanic* sank.

The name *Gigantic* would of course have fitted better with the names of the first two ships of the Class, which were named after the Greek immortal races, the Olympians and the Titans, with the addition of White Star's suffix '–ic', used on all their ships (had they been Cunard ships they would have been the *Olympia* and the *Titania*, as Cunard used the suffix '-ia'). The name *Gigantic* is derived from the Giants, who like the Titans were defeated in battle by the Olympian gods. This coincidentally echoes the careers of the three ships, as *Britannic* sank during the First World War and therefore only the *Olympic* survived, eventually being scrapped in 1935. As early as 1st June, 1911, the morning after *Titanic's* launch, the editor of the *Irish News* and *Belfast Morning News* questioned the choice of her name, pointing out that Zeus '...smote the strong and daring Titans with thunderbolts; and their final abiding place was in some limbo beneath the lowest depths of the Tartarus.'

5 TITANIC'S OWNERS WERE TRYING TO SAVE MONEY IN HER CONSTRUCTION, CAUSING THEM TO CUT CORNERS ON QUALITY AND SAFETY.

No. The *Olympic*-class was the White Star Line's answer to the revolution in shipbuilding brought by Cunard with the *Mauretania* class. The White Star Line hoped to make a profit, certainly, but with the aim of creating the latest in transatlantic comfort and luxury; too much cost-cutting would have been a false economy. As Joseph Bruce Ismay, Chairman of the White Star Line, explained at the US enquiry into the sinking:

> JBI013: '*Titanic* was the latest thing in the art of shipbuilding; absolutely no money was spared in her construction. She was not built by contract. She was simply built on a commission.'

This meant that *Titanic* was built on a 'cost plus' basis, where profit for the builders was calculated by adding an agreed amount to the costs they incurred in building her, leaving them with no incentive to cut costs. Indeed, Lord Pirrie, who owned *Titanic*'s builders, Harland and Wolff, in Belfast, was also a part owner of the White Star Line, *Titanic*'s owners.

It is also worth mentioning that the *Olympic*, the first in her class and therefore potentially the most susceptible to design faults, served successfully from 1911 to 1935 and was later known as 'Old Reliable', having acted as a troop carrier throughout the First World War. She was also the only merchant ship to ram and sink a German U-boat, and before *Titanic* sank had already survived a collision with HMS *Hawke* which snapped off the Navy ship's battering ram—a record which ought to dispel any accusations of poor quality construction.

6 REGULATIONS STATED THAT THERE SHOULD BE ENOUGH LIFEBOATS FOR EVERYONE ON BOARD.

No. Before the *Titanic* disaster, lifeboats for all were not required on passenger liners, in cases where these ships were efficiently sub-divided into watertight compartments.

The White Star Line had in fact provided more lifesaving equipment than the Board of Trade regulations required. For any ship with a gross register tonnage of over 10,000, only 16 lifeboats were required. *Titanic* complied with this requirement because she carried 14 standard lifeboats with a capacity of 65 persons each, and two emergency lifeboats with a capacity of 40 persons each, making 16 lifeboats in total. She also carried four Englehardt collapsible boats, with a capacity of 47 each. *Titanic* therefore carried a total of 20 boats, with a total carrying capacity of 1,178 people, or room for 216 more people than the Board of Trade rules stipulated at that time. However, she was certified to carry 3,547 passengers and crew.

Nor did large and properly subdivided passenger liners in Europe and America carry enough lifeboats for all their passengers. For example, one of the five large German ships the court considered was the passenger liner *Berlin*, which had a Gross Register Tonnage of 17,324 and was licensed to carry 2,690 persons; but only had 24 lifeboats, which could only accommodate 48% of her passengers.

However, the Board of Trade did require cargo steamers, which were smaller, not properly subdivided, and which carried far fewer people, to provide enough lifeboats for everyone, on both sides of the ship, because they realised that in almost all situations where lifeboats would be needed, a list to port or starboard, or the direction of the sea, would make launching the lifeboats on one side of the ship impossible. For a large passenger liner like *Titanic*, though, this would have meant carrying 92 lifeboats (46 on each side of the ship) which would seriously affect stability, take up most of the deck space and be practically impossible to launch in most emergency situations, not least due to the lack of trained crew required to man so many boats.

Sir Norman Hill, Chairman of the merchant ship advisory committee, said that it was practically impossible for an 'emigrant ship' to have boats for all, and that moreover the statistics showed that it wouldn't make much difference:

> 24652: (The Commissioner) 'Then it comes to this, does it Sir Norman, that it is practically impossible for an emigrant ship designed to carry 2,000 people, to carry lifeboats sufficient to hold those 2,000 people at one time?'
>
> 'With lifeboats readily available for launching, it is an absolute impossibility, I believe. Now, My Lord, if that is an unsafe ship then you could prohibit her sailing the seas; but our view is (and of course we had before us the records of these boats year after year, we have had in detail the 20 years' record) that we cannot say that that is an unsafe ship. If you compare the loss of life on that class of ship with a cargo-boat trading across the North Atlantic, with boat accommodation on each side for everybody on board, the loss of life in the emigrant ship, both amongst the crew and amongst the passengers, is a bagatelle compared with the loss of life on the other boat.'

Indeed, out of 32,000 trans-Atlantic voyages in the 20 years preceding the *Titanic* disaster, there had been only 25 cases in which either the ship had been lost, or lives had been lost.

The total number of deaths was only 148—68 passengers and 80 crew. The vast majority of ships crossing the Atlantic in this period were passenger ships, so these figures indicate just how safe the passenger trade had been up to the point when *Titanic* sank, and why the lack of lifeboats was not felt to be a problem. White Star Line's general manager, Harold Sanderson, estimated that, 'nineteen times out of twenty', lifeboats could not be lowered safely in an emergency situation.

Furthermore, the shipping lanes themselves had been separated between eastbound and westbound in order to avoid collisions; and it was regarded that these lanes were so busy that rescue ships would always be near to hand.

For all of these reasons, the Board of Trade concluded that the onus for large passenger vessels should be on increasing watertight subdivision to keep vessels afloat, rather than on increasing the number of lifeboats, which would be unlikely to save an increased number of passengers in most disaster situations and which were generally only regarded as useful for ferrying passengers to rescue ships standing nearby.

With the benefit of the hindsight which the *Titanic* disaster has afforded us, we can see that the Board of Trade was wrong in coming to these conclusions. This is perhaps not surprising when one realises that they took their lead from the Merchant Ship Advisory Committee, which was dominated by ship owners, who were alert to the cost implications of providing boats for all on their passenger fleets, and whose passengers liked spacious deck areas for recreation.

7 TITANIC'S OWNERS OPPOSED THE ADDITION OF MORE
LIFEBOATS, IN ORDER TO GIVE PASSENGERS MORE ROOM ON
THE PROMENADE DECKS.

Yes. The White Star Line knew that the Board of Trade was
about to change the regulations, and they thought that they
might be required to carry more lifeboats, so Double Acting
Quadrant Welin davits, which could carry several lifeboats
each, were fitted. *Titanic* was even fitted with boat chocks in
her deck to carry 64 lifeboats, if necessary. However, Bruce
Ismay, Chairman of the White Star Line, didn't see any
need to put more boats on until they were required by these
new regulations, especially as open promenade decks were a
selling point, and these had been made even more spacious
on the *Olympic* Class liners, due to their revolutionary new
ventilation designs, which meant they could eliminate the
unsightly deck cowls which crowded the decks of their
Cunard rivals. The *Olympic* Class liners had achieved this by
making the fourth funnel purely a ventilation shaft, rather
than a true funnel taking smoke away from the boilers.

It is often said that Alexander Carlisle, brother-in-law of
Harland & Wolff's Chairman, Lord Pirrie, and Managing
Director of the yard, before Thomas Andrews took over that
position, urged Ismay to carry additional boats. Indeed, in
an interview with the *Daily Mail* on April 18th, 1912 he said
'As ships grew bigger, I was always in favour of increasing the
lifeboat accommodation'. However, it seems he never told
Bruce Ismay this because, as he revealed later in the same
interview: 'If any ships had been fitted with the full number
of lifeboats I proposed, it would no doubt have set up an

invidious situation with respect to the steamers of all lines now trading in the North Atlantic. It would have drawn attention.'

As it turns out, the regulations which would have come into force if *Titanic* had not sunk might actually have required ships like *Titanic* to carry fewer lifeboats, as the proposal was to further connect lifeboat provision to efficient watertight subdivision.

Ismay's view that they didn't need more lifeboats didn't arise from a reckless disregard for safety or a foolish desire to have a more attractive ship at the expense of more essential features. His opinion of lifeboats was shared by others of the time, such as Captain Rostron of the *Carpathia*, *Titanic*'s rescue ship:

AHR111: (Senator Smith) 'Are these regulations of the British Board of Trade new regulations or old regulations?'

'They are of recent date.'

AHR112: 'The fact that, under these regulations, you are obliged to carry 20 lifeboats and the *Titanic* was only obliged to carry 20, with her additional tonnage, indicates either that these regulations were prescribed long ago—'

(Rostron, interposing): 'No, sir; it has nothing to do with that. What it has to do with is the ship itself. The ships are built nowadays to be practically unsinkable, and each ship is supposed to be a lifeboat in itself. The boats are merely supposed to be put on as a standby. The ships are supposed to be built, and the naval architects say they are, unsinkable under certain conditions. What the exact conditions are, I do not know, as to whether it is with alternate compartments full, or what it may be. That is why in our ship we carry more lifeboats, for the simple reason that we are built differently from the *Titanic*; differently constructed.'

Nevertheless, following the *Titanic* disaster Ismay personally ordered that all ships owned by the International Mercantile Marine, White Star Line's parent company, should carry lifeboats for all.

Omens

8 THE TITANIC DISASTER WAS PREDICTED 14 YEARS BEFORE IT HAPPENED BY WRITER MORGAN ROBERTSON.

Yes. In his 1898 novella entitled *Futility, or the Wreck of the Titan*, Robertson told the story of a 'superliner' named the *Titan*, which sank after striking an iceberg on a calm April night, with great loss of life. The *Titan* was 'the largest craft afloat and the greatest of the works of men'. Also like the *Titanic*, she had new watertight compartments which could be closed from the bridge in an instant, and was considered 'practically unsinkable', as she could float with nine of her watertight compartments flooded, and no accident could be imagined which would flood more. Nor did the *Titan* carry enough lifeboats for everyone on board.

The novella's plot does differ in some respects from the real-life disaster—the *Titan* capsized and sank very quickly on her third trip from New York, and the ship's specifications aren't exactly the same, but the similarities are nevertheless striking. Indeed, *Titanic*'s sinking on her *maiden* voyage is a good example of the truth being stranger than fiction, and this may explain some of our enduring fascination with the disaster.

Robertson's novella also parallels incidents involving the *Olympic*; the *Titan* sinks a smaller ship in a collision, just as the *Olympic* rammed and sank the Nantucket lightship in fog in the 1930s.

In 1914, Robertson again demonstrated his extraordinary powers of prediction in his short story *Beyond the Spectrum*, about a war between the Americans and the Japanese which began with a sneak attack by the Japanese on Hawaii and involved the use of a searchlight developed by the Americans which had similar effects to the atomic bomb, including blindness, heat and facial burns.

9 CATHOLIC WORKERS AT HARLAND & WOLFF SABOTAGED TITANIC BECAUSE HER HULL NUMBER WAS ANTI-CATHOLIC.

No. This myth is based on the mistaken belief that *Titanic*'s hull number was 3909 04 which, if seen reflected, could be made out as spelling 'No Pope'. However, this number has no connection with the *Titanic*, which had a hull number of 401 and a Board of Trade registration number of 131,428. There is also no evidence of sabotage; *Titanic* did not need to be sabotaged in order to be sunk by the collision.

It's true that Protestant-Catholic relations were very bad in Ireland at that time but Lord Pirrie, although a supporter of Home Rule, would not have tolerated major disputes which interfered with the work of the Yard. The shipyards were in a Protestant area of Belfast, and there would probably have been anti-Home Rule slogans chalked up around the yard, but there was no reason to associate these with the *Titanic* in particular.

IO A WORKER WAS ACCIDENTALLY SEALED INTO TITANIC'S HULL
WHEN SHE WAS UNDER CONSTRUCTION IN BELFAST.

No, although stories of Isambard Kingdom Brunel's ship, the
Great Eastern, suggest that this myth may have originated
there, where boys were required to work in the narrow
space between her double hulls, where only they could fit.
Later, men working on the ship complained of mysterious
hammering noises below decks, which they said were the
ghosts of those boys who had been trapped inside. It was
also claimed that skeletal remains were found inside her hull
when the Great Eastern was broken up for scrap, but there
is no contemporary report of this, and the hull was never
actually sealed, having several hatches for access.

The *Great Eastern* (at that time called *Leviathan*) may not
have been haunted, but she was beset with difficulties in her
construction and lifetime.

On her sea trials, there was an explosion in her boiler
room which killed several people, and on one voyage from
New York she ran down and damaged a small sailing ship,
the *Jane*. She also collided with a rock off Long Island, an
accident which ripped a gash in her outer hull 9 feet wide by
83 feet long, over 60 times the area of *Titanic*'s damage. Her
double hull, however, allowed her to reach harbour with only
a list to port to show for the damage. Interestingly, *Titanic*
would also have survived this accident, as a continuous tear
of 83 feet in the forward part of her hull would not have
flooded more than three of *Titanic*'s forward compartments
and *Titanic* was designed to cope with this sort of injury.
Unluckily for *Titanic*, her much smaller injury was spread

over a much greater length of her hull—300 feet—thus breaching the first six of her watertight compartments.

Although *Great Eastern* was unsuccessful as a commercial ship and inefficient in many ways, history has shown us that Brunel was nevertheless greatly ahead of his time when he finally launched her in 1858. Indeed, Brunel's 19,000 ton, 700 feet long *Great Eastern*, launched in 1858, is probably still the closest the world has ever got to a truly unsinkable ship. Like *Titanic*, she had 15 transverse watertight bulkheads, but hers had no doors in them, went higher, and joined a watertight bulkhead deck at the top. *Great Eastern* also had a complete double-hull, but *Titanic*'s double bottom did not extend much higher than the turn of her bilges.

11 TITANIC'S CONSTRUCTION, LAUNCH AND SAILING WERE PLAGUED BY BAD LUCK.

No, although it is easy to see how this rumour developed, with the benefit of hindsight. Working in a shipyard in 1912 was undoubtedly dangerous, and at least one worker was killed during *Titanic*'s construction: James Dobbins, 43, whose legs were pinned by a support he was cutting during her launch. His friends dragged him to safety and he was taken to hospital, but he died the next day.

Unsurprisingly, many people claimed after the disaster that they had 'known' she was going to sink, or had a 'strange feeling' about the ship. For example, the fashion designer Lady Duff Gordon remembered in her memoirs, written years later, a 'curious reluctance' to cross on the new ship when told that the only berths available for her urgent business trip were on the *Titanic*; the booking clerk reassured her with tales of the ship's supposed unsinkability. *Titanic* survivor Esther Hart refused to sleep during the voyage, as she felt that something bad would happen to the ship. As a result, she was awake when disaster struck and managed to get herself and her daughter Eva into a lifeboat, although Eva's father died in the sinking.

However, it is not surprising that with 711 survivors, one or two of them would have remembered feeling nervous about sailing beforehand. At least two stories claimed that the ship's fate could be seen in omens during her launch and sailing, such as the story that the figure of Death appeared above the ship as she left Queenstown (now Cobh) in Ireland, the last port before beginning the Atlantic crossing. This was no more than one of the stokers, with a blackened face from working the coal, climbing up inside *Titanic*'s ventilation funnel to admire the view.

Another of these 'omens' claimed that the bottle failed to break against her hull when she was christened, which is generally taken to mean bad luck for the ship. In fact, the White Star Line never christened their ships, and so *Titanic* never had a champagne bottle smashed against her hull. 'They just builds 'er and shoves 'er in,' as a shipyard worker explained at the time. The 1958 film *A Night to Remember* incorrectly shows *Titanic* being christened, using footage from the launch of Cunard's *Queen Elizabeth* in 1938.

Following the disaster, people pointed to these incidents, along with *Titanic*'s near collision with the *New York* as she left

Southampton harbour, and said that *Titanic*'s maiden voyage was cursed. Sailors are notoriously superstitious, and this and other incidents may have caused even *Titanic*'s officers to feel that she was not a 'happy ship'. For example, Second Officer Bisset of the *Carpathia* recalled in his memoirs *Tramps and Ladies* that when Captain Rostron asked the *Titanic*'s rescued Fourth Officer Boxhall: 'Where is the *Titanic*?' Boxhall replied: 'Gone, she was Hoodooed from the start.'

12 TITANIC WAS SUNK BY A MUMMY'S CURSE.

No, and there is no evidence that any mummy was ever put on board the *Titanic*. The mummy tale, in a slightly different form, was originally invented by *Titanic* passenger W.T. Stead, a well-known liberal, journalist and paranormal investigator, and his friend Douglas Murray. Stead, a lifelong campaigner for peace, was travelling to New York at the request of US President Howard Taft to speak at a peace congress at Carnegie Hall; he lost his life when the ship went down.

The pair invented a tale about a mummy recently brought back to England by a friend of theirs, claiming that it brought havoc and destruction wherever it went. The story goes that the mummy had been dug up at the end of the 19th century in Luxor and offered for sale to four Englishmen, who drew lots for its purchase. All four men suffered accidents and misfortunes, some fatal, and the mummy continued to cause death and destruction wherever it went. After visiting the

British Museum and seeing the anguished expression of the priestess of Amun-Ra's painted face on her sarcophagus lid, they came up with another story about her evil spirit being loose in the world. Stead and Murray told both these stories to the press and they were conflated. Some years later, Stead related them with much relish to his dinner companions on the *Titanic* on the night of April 12th, 1912, allegedly drawing out his narrative till just after midnight on the 13th. At this point it seems that the Amun-Ra story was only about the sarcophagus lid, rather than the mummy itself.

After the disaster, Frederic Seward, the only surviving dinner companion who had heard Stead's tales, recounted the story of the dinner for a book about the stories of survivors. The tale, already reported and embroidered, became associated with the *Titanic* through the Stead connection and a new version was invented which claimed that the mummy had in fact been on board and had sunk the ship. In this version, the British Museum sold it to an American who didn't believe tales of the curse and arranged to have it shipped back to America in April 1912 on White Star Line's brand new ship *Titanic*. The rest, as they say, is history, although, in an added detail, the mummy was apparently rescued in a lifeboat and smuggled aboard the *Carpathia* (no explanation is offered as to how this might have been done). When its new owner became convinced, owing to a series of accidents, that it really was cursed, he arranged to have it transferred to Canada and shipped back to Britain on the *Empress of Ireland*, which duly sank in May 1914.

Maiden Voyage

13 TITANIC WAS FILLED TO CAPACITY ON HER MAIDEN VOYAGE.

No. *Titanic* was only about half full as she carried approximately 1,308 passengers on her maiden voyage, but had the capacity to carry 2,603. Some passengers may have decided to travel on the *Titanic* because of the popularity of Captain E.J.Smith, known as the 'Millionaire's Captain', for his reputation as an experienced and debonair commander of transatlantic liners, or because of the class's reputation for comfort. The Dodge family, according to Walter Lord, had been persuaded by their steward on the *Olympic*, *Titanic's* sister ship, to travel back to America on the *Titanic*. For many, though, it would simply have been the first available or convenient choice. Lady Duff Gordon, who booked at the last minute for an urgent business trip to the New York branch of her fashion house, Maison Lucile, was still able to obtain First Class cabins for herself and her husband, Sir Cosmo.

However, due to a miners' strike, which had only just ended on April 6th, there was a general shortage of coal; arrangements had been made with other shipping Lines to transfer their coal to *Titanic*, and to transfer their passengers who had booked on other ships to sail on *Titanic's* maiden voyage. These passengers therefore did not choose to travel on the *Titanic*, but would have almost certainly been pleased to be transferred to a newer and more comfortable ship. A number of berths were filled this way, but even with these extra passengers *Titanic* was only half-full.

This was also the case for *Titanic*'s older sister, *Olympic*, on her maiden voyage. She was also only a little over half-full, but the 425 First Class passengers she carried on that trip was considered to be a record for a westward voyage in June, even though the *Olympic*-class had the capacity for over 900 passengers in First Class.

14 TITANIC WAS ON FIRE WHEN SHE LEFT SOUTHAMPTON.

Yes. The fire may have started as early as Tuesday 2nd April, when the *Titanic* was still in Belfast, in the coal bunker between No. 5 and No. 6 boiler rooms. The crew began to extinguish the fire by raking the burning coal out of the bunker during their first watch after leaving Southampton on Wednesday 10th April, 1912, but the fire was not completely extinguished until Saturday 13th April, as testified by Fireman Charles Hendrickson:

> 5232: 'Do you remember a fire in a coal bunker on board this boat?'
> 'Yes.'
> 5233: 'Is it a common occurrence for fires to take place on boats?'

'No.'

5234: 'It is not common?'

'No.'

5235: 'How long have you been on a White Star boat?'

'About five years.'

5236: 'When did you last see a fire in a coal bunker?'

'I never saw one before.'

5237: 'It has been suggested that fires in coal bunkers are quite a common occurrence, but you have been five years in the White Star line and have not seen a fire in a coal bunker?'

'No.'

5238: 'Did you help to get the coal out?'

'Yes.'

5239: 'Did you hear when the fire commenced?'

'Yes, I heard it commenced at Belfast.'

5240: 'When did you start getting the coal out?'

'The first watch we did from Southampton we started to get it out.'

5241: 'How many days would that be after you left Belfast?'

'I do not know when she left Belfast to the day.'

5242: 'It would be two or three days, I suppose?'

'I should say so.'

5243: 'Did it take much time to get the fire down?'

'It took us right up to the Saturday to get it out.'

5244: 'How long did it take to put the fire itself out?'

'The fire was not out much before all the coal was out.'

5245: 'The fire was not extinguished until you got the whole of the coal out?'

'No. I finished the bunker out myself, me and three or four men that were there. We worked everything out.'

5246: 'The bulkhead forms part of the bunker—the side?

'Yes, you could see where the bulkhead had been red hot.'

5247: 'You looked at the side after the coal had been taken out?'

'Yes.'

5248: 'What condition was it in?'

'You could see where it had been red hot; all the paint and everything was off. It was dented a bit.'

5249. 'It was damaged, at any rate?'

'Yes, warped.'

5250: 'Was much notice taken of it. Was any attempt made to do anything with it?'

'I just brushed it off and got some black oil and rubbed over it.'

5251: 'To give it its ordinary appearance?'

'Yes.'

Maurice Clark, Assistant Emigration Officer at the Board of Trade, inspected *Titanic* on Wednesday morning, 10th April, and failed to spot this fire. He said that it had not been reported to him and claimed that such fires were not unusual:

24119: 'Was there any report made to you about a fire having taken place in the bunker in Section 5?'

'No.'

24120: 'In the ordinary case ought such a report to have been made to you if there was a serious fire before the ship sailed?'

'Yes, if it was a serious fire it ought to have been reported to me.'

24121: 'If it was sufficiently serious for it to be reported—if it was regarded as so serious by the Officer that it ought to be reported to the makers, would it, in your view, be sufficiently serious for a report to be made to you?'

'Hardly, it is not an uncommon thing to have these small fires in the bunkers.'

Lightoller tried to portray the Inspector, Captain Clark, as a martinet, over-diligent in his duties, but it seems that this may have been one opportunity to stop *Titanic* leaving on her fatal maiden voyage, which was missed by the incompetent Board of Trade. As Captain Clark himself admitted at the British Inquiry, although this discussion was specifically dealing with poor lifeboat drills:

24166: 'Then you do not think your system before this disaster was satisfactory?'

'No, not very satisfactory.'

24167: 'Well, was it satisfactory?'

'Well, I think we might with advantage—'

24168: 'Will you answer the question: was it

satisfactory?'

'No.'

24169: 'It was your plan, nevertheless?'

'My plan? No, it is the custom.'

24170: 'Never mind about the custom; it is what you did?'

'Yes.'

24171: 'And you now do not think it is satisfactory?'

'No.'

24172. 'Did you think it satisfactory before the *Titanic* accident?'

'Well, no.'

24173: 'Then why did you do it?'

'Because it is the custom.'

24174: 'But do you follow custom, although it is bad?'

'Well, you will remember I am a Civil Servant. Custom guides us a good bit.'

(The Commissioner): 'Perhaps that is the answer.'

Although the fire made the bulkhead glow hot and left it slightly warped, naval architect Edward Wilding, one of *Titanic*'s designers, was very definite that despite its location, the fire wouldn't have seriously damaged the bulkhead or contributed to the sinking. Although he had not seen the fire himself, he said that it would have to be much more serious than anything that had been described to destroy the bulkhead's watertight properties:

20409: 'Now, just to clear up one matter about the

bulkhead between No. 5 and 6 boiler section. You know there has been some confusion about a hole there, an injury to the bulkhead. Just tell me, you have heard this fire in the bulkhead described?'

'I have.'

20410: 'In your judgment would that injure the bulkhead as a watertight arrangement?'

'Not materially. The evidence as to the actual character of the fire has not been very definite, but it would have to be a much more alarming fire than anything that has been described to destroy the watertightness of the bulkhead. It might weep very slightly a few bucketsfull an hour, that could easily be handled by the pumps.'

20411: 'It did not materially affect it?'

'Not materially.'

15 TITANIC WAS CARRYING GOLD BULLION.

No, this is a myth in the case of the *Titanic*, although in 1917 the White Star liner *Laurentic* was sunk off the coast of Northern Ireland carrying 35 tons of gold ingots. These were worth £5 million at the time (about £250 million today) and were destined for the purchase of munitions from America, which at that time had not yet entered the First World War. All but 22 of these ingots were recovered by Royal Navy divers between 1917 and 1924.

The most valuable items aboard the *Titanic* were the

personal effects of the first class passengers, many of which were lost in the sinking. These included a jewelled copy of the *Rubaiyat of Omar Khayyam*; a 35-hp Renault car belonging to First Class passenger William Carter Sr; and a 16th-century second edition of essays by Francis Bacon, owned by Harry Widener, a 1907 Harvard graduate whose mother Eleanor subsequently endowed the Widener Memorial Library at the college in his memory. Eleanor herself owned a valuable string of pearls, but she wore them off the ship, as the Countess of Rothes did with the pearls given to her on her wedding day.

Titanic's passengers did not always make the obvious choice that night regarding the items they wanted to save. First Class passenger Major Arthur Peuchen left a box with $300,000 in cash and preferred bonds in his cabin, taking instead a good luck pin and three oranges. Edith Russell ran back to her cabin to fetch her 'lucky pig', a musical box which she always took with her when travelling; and Margaret 'Molly' Brown had an Egyptian figurine in her pocket, which she carried as a good luck charm. She later presented this to Captain Rostron on board the Carpathia.

Following the *Titanic* disaster, damages claims from survivors totalled $16 million, though a considerable part of this sum was claimed for loss of life, rather than merely possessions. In the end, partly guided by the principle of Limited Liability for shipowners, White Star agreed with the claimants to settle all claims for a payment of only $664,000. The litigation had taken more than four years.

16 TITANIC NEARLY COLLIDED WITH ANOTHER SHIP AS SHE
LEFT SOUTHAMPTON.

Yes. This incident is brilliantly described in the following passage
from *Titanic and other Ships*, the memoirs of *Titanic's* Second
Officer, Charles Herbert Lightoller, published in 1935:

'Before she cleared the dock we had a striking example
of the power that lay in those engines and propellers.
    'The *Oceanic* and *St Paul* [sic: it was in fact *St Paul's*
sister ship, the *New York*] were lying moored to the
wharf alongside each other. They happened to be in a
position where the *Titanic* had to make a slight turn,
which necessitated coming astern on her port engine.
The terrific suction set up in that shallow water,
simply dragged both these great liners away from the
wharf. The *St Paul* [sic] broke adrift altogether, and
the *Oceanic* was dragged off until a sixty foot gangway
dropped from the wharf into the water. It looked as
if nothing could save the *St Paul* [sic] crashing into
Titanic's stern, in fact, it was only Captain Smith's
experience and resource that saved her. The *Titanic*, of
course, dwarfed these two ships, and made them look
like cross-channel boats, and the wash from her screws
had a corresponding influence. Just as a collision
seemed inevitable, Captain Smith gave the *Titanic* a
touch ahead on her port engine, which simply washed
the *St Paul* [sic] away, and kept her clear until a couple
of tugs, to our unbounded relief, got hold, and took
her back alongside the wharf.

'The greatest care had to be taken whilst threading our way down the then comparatively shallow channel of Southampton Water and eventually out to Spithead. There was a general feeling of relief when at last we got her into her proper element, deep water.'

It is ironic to think that, had Captain Smith not averted a collision by his skill on this occasion, *Titanic*'s maiden voyage would either have been delayed by several hours or cancelled altogether, meaning that either she would have encountered ice during daylight, or she would have been travelling slightly later in the year, when everyone would have been aware of the incredible extent of the ice blocking the westbound track to New York at that time, and the fatal encounter would never have taken place.

17 CAPTAIN SMITH WAS ACCIDENT PRONE.

Yes, but only in this new class of liner. Captain Smith had not become one of the most successful and highly paid liner captains in the world by being accident prone. He had over 40 years' experience at sea and was regarded as a very skilled handler of ships, as we have seen. As Lightoller points out in his memoirs, *Titanic and Other Ships*:

'Captain E.J. was one of the ablest Skippers on the Atlantic, and accusations of recklessness, carelessness, not taking due precautions, or driving his ship at too high a speed, were absolutely, and utterly unfounded; but the armchair complaint is a very common disease.'

However, *Titanic* and *Olympic,* at over 45,000 GRT, were nearly twice the size of Smith's previous command, the 24,541 GRT *Adriatic,* which Smith had captained since her maiden voyage in 1907. As we saw in the previous question, these giant new *Olympic* class liners had handling characteristics with which no-one at the time was familiar, not even Captain Smith.

Although technically under pilot at the time, this explains why Smith experienced an unusual number of accidents with these giant new ships, and not just *Titanic*'s near-miss with the *New York*. At 12.46 p.m. on September 20th, 1911, the same hydrodynamic forces associated with this new class of ship caused the *Olympic* to suck into her side the 7,500-ton Royal Navy cruiser HMS *Hawke*. Both ships were doing about 15 knots and were only about 200 yards apart at the time, as they were leaving Southampton down the narrow channel of water called Spithead, off the Isle of Wight. HMS *Hawke*'s prow and battering ram pierced the *Olympic*'s hull both above and below the waterline on *Olympic*'s starboard quarter near her stern, flooding two compartments and damaging her starboard propeller. Her voyage to New York had to be cancelled and her passengers taken off by tender. *Olympic* then limped back to Southampton and later to Belfast for six weeks of repairs, which delayed *Titanic*'s completion.

Captain Smith even had two small accidents with

Olympic on her maiden voyage. As she was arriving in New York on June 21st, 1911, one of the 12 tugs nursing her into her slip at the especially lengthened Pier 59, the tug *O. L. Hallenbeck*, was sucked against *Olympic*'s stern by a burst of reverse thrust from *Olympic*'s starboard propeller, cutting off the *Hallenbeck*'s stern frame, rudder, and wheel shaft. *Olympic* also scraped the corner of the dock in New York, on her way into the slip.

Regardless of Captain Smith's undoubted great skill and experience, these giant liners simply behaved differently; indeed, it was *Titanic*'s sheer size that made her glancing blow with the iceberg fatal, as her Second Officer also explains in his 1935 memoirs:

'She struck the berg well forward of the foremast, and evidently there had been a slight shelf protruding below the water. This pierced her bow as she threw her whole weight on the ice, some actually falling on her fore deck. The impact flung her bow off, but only by the whip or spring of the ship. Again she struck, this time a little further aft. Each blow stove in a plate, below the water line, as the ship had not the inherent strength to resist.

'Had it been, for instance, the old *Majestic* or even the *Oceanic* the chances are that either of them would have been strong enough to take the blow and be bodily thrown off without serious damage. For instance, coming alongside with the old *Majestic*, it was no uncommon thing for her to hit a knuckle of the wharf a good healthy bump, but beyond, perhaps, scraping off the paint, no damage was ever done. The same, to a lesser extent with the *Oceanic*.

'Then ships grew in size, out of all proportion to their strength, till one would see a modern liner brought with all the skill and care possible, fall slowly, and ever so gently on a knuckle, to bend and dent a plate like a piece of tin.

'That is exactly what happened to the *Titanic*. She just bump, bump, bumped along the berg, holing herself each time, till she was making water in no less than six compartments, though, unfortunately, we were not to know this until much later.'

Captain Smith had not been accident prone, or unskilled, or careless, but these were ships of a different era and neither he nor anyone else had any experience in handling such enormous vessels.

18 TITANIC WAS TRYING TO WIN THE BLUE RIBAND FOR THE FASTEST ATLANTIC CROSSING.

No. As we have seen, *Titanic* could never have achieved this. She was not the fastest liner, nor was she intended to be, and the speed record set by *Mauretania* in 1909 remained unbroken until 1929.

However, there is evidence that *Titanic* was trying to beat *Olympic's* maiden voyage crossing time and arrive in New

York on Tuesday night, instead of Wednesday morning as advertised. This would have been a major public relations boost for the second sister, and therefore highly desirable from the point of view of her owners.

In her 22nd November, 1913 deposition for the Limited Liability Hearings into the disaster, First Class passenger Elisabeth Lines remembered a conversation between White Star Line Chairman J. Bruce Ismay and Captain Smith on Saturday 13th April in which Ismay pointed out that *Titanic* was making good time, had already matched the *Olympic*'s maiden voyage run and, with a little extra speed could 'beat the *Olympic* and get into New York on Tuesday'. Mrs Lines was quite definite about this statement, which she was asked in questioning to repeat three times. She also remembered that Ismay had seemed 'emphatic' that the *Titanic* was performing as well as or better than the *Olympic* and he was therefore confident that she could reach New York on Tuesday night:

35: 'Would you be good enough to state when it was on Saturday April thirteenth that this conversation occurred?'

'After the midday meal I went into the lounge to have my coffee—in the general reception room.'

36: 'Were the Captain and Mr. Ismay already there?'

'No, they came in after I was seated, and went to this same table which I had seen them occupy on the Friday.'

37: 'Could you estimate about what time it was that the Captain and Mr. Ismay entered the reception room or lounge?'

'Perhaps half past one.'

39: 'About how long, within your knowledge, did Mr. Ismay and Captain Smith remain in this reception room engaged in conversation?'

'At least two hours.'

40: 'Were you there all of that time?'

'I was there.'

41: 'Are you able to state from your recollection the words that you heard spoken between Mr. Ismay and Captain Smith on that occasion?'

'We had had a very good run. At first I did not pay any attention to what they were saying, they were simply talking and I was occupied, and then my attention was arrested by hearing the day's run discussed, which I already knew had been a very good one in the preceeding [sic] twenty-four hours, and I heard Mr. Ismay—it was Mr. Ismay who did the talking—I heard him give the length of the run, and I heard him say, "Well, we did better to-day than we did yesterday, we made a better run to-day than we did yesterday, we will make a better run to-morrow. Things are working smoothly, the machinery is bearing the test, the boilers are working well." They went on discussing it, and then I heard him make the statement: "We will beat the *Olympic* and get in to New York on Tuesday."'

53: 'What would you say as to your ability to hear all that was said in an ordinary tone of voice between Captain Smith and Mr. Ismay in the positions in which they were and you were on that afternoon of Saturday?

'It was quite possible, as during the latter part of the time there were very few people left in the lounge and it was quiet.'

56: 'And what runs of the *Olympic* were they using as a comparison?'

'The trial trip.'

57: 'Do you mean the maiden voyage?'

'Yes, the maiden voyage.'

58: 'And what was the substance or the words if you can give them, of the conversation as regards the *Olympic*?'

'It was comparison, and that the *Titanic* was doing equally well, and they seemed to think a little more pressure could be put on the boilers and the speed increased so that the maiden trip of the *Titanic* would exceed the maiden trip of the *Olympic* in speed.'

However, Ismay denied this in his testimony at the British inquiry into the sinking, held in May 1912. Ismay admitted to having had a conversation with *Titanic*'s chief engineer, Joseph Bell, when *Titanic* was at Queenstown (now Cobh, Ireland) on Thursday 11th April, but he dismissed the idea that they had been discussing *Titanic* arriving at New York on the Tuesday evening, saying it was impossible, and that in any case, with the coal strike they wished to conserve fuel and would therefore not intend to drive her at full speed except for a short period on the Monday or Tuesday.

This echoes Captain Smith's response in the *New York*

Times of June 22nd, 1911, after the *Olympic*'s maiden voyage, when he was asked, 'Will she ever dock on Tuesday?' 'No,' he replied emphatically, 'and there will be no attempt to bring her in on Tuesday. She was built for a Wednesday ship, and her run this first voyage has demonstrated that she will fulfill the expectations of the builders.' However, on her very next crossing to New York, Olympic did arrive on Tuesday night.

Given Mrs Lines' clear remembrance of the conversation, which also included a discussion of running the ship at full speed on the Monday, the fact that the *Olympic* had already managed a Tuesday arrival, and the figures for *Titanic*'s run up to the point of her collision, which show that with only 62% of her maiden voyage completed, she had already equalled *Olympic*'s average speed for her entire maiden voyage, it seems very likely that Ismay was trying to bring *Titanic* in early. His recollection of events at Queenstown need not have been an outright lie; it is possible he wanted to see how well she would do before deciding for certain that he would try for a Tuesday night arrival in New York, thus avoiding embarrassment if it proved impossible in the event—which would account for his later discussion with Captain Smith, which Mrs Lines recalled, about the ship's speed and distance covered so far.

Had she not collided with an iceberg, *Titanic* quite probably would have arrived in New York on Tuesday evening, thus beating her sister's maiden voyage time. In the event, the second sister got more publicity than even Ismay had hoped for, but for all the wrong reasons.

19 TITANIC WAS SHORT OF COAL, BECAUSE OF A COAL STRIKE.

No, although Ismay mentioned this to defend himself against charges of speeding and there was a shortage of coal at that time, due to a miners' strike. This strike, according to the Lloyds' Weekly Shipping Index, ended on 6th April, 1912, but with *Titanic* due to sail on the 10th, preparations had already been made to provide her with enough coal; as we have seen, other ships gave up their allowance to enable *Titanic* to make her voyage, and passengers were accordingly transferred from these ships onto the *Titanic*. The idea that the *Titanic* was short of coal was spread by the White Star Line at the Inquiries into the disaster following *Titanic*'s collision, where it was used by Bruce Ismay and Third Officer Herbert Pitman, among others, to imply that *Titanic* could not have been travelling at full speed, as she did not have enough coal to reach New York at anything like full speed.

The reality is that, prior to *Titanic*'s maiden voyage on Wednesday 10th April, 1912, Captain Maurice Clark of The Board of Trade had certified that:

> 'The coal on board is certified to amount to 5,892 tons, which is sufficient to take the ship to her next coaling port.'

This meant *Titanic* was in fact carrying 1,000 tons more coal than the *Olympic* did on her maiden voyage the year before, when she arrived in New York with 1,300 tons to spare.

20 OWNER ISMAY ACTED AS A 'SUPER-CAPTAIN' AND ORDERED CAPTAIN SMITH TO MAINTAIN FULL SPEED DESPITE THE UNUSUAL ICE WARNINGS THEY HAD RECEIVED.

No. We have seen that Ismay did urge Captain Smith to get into New York early; and we know that Ismay discussed the speed of the *Titanic* with Chief Engineer bell at Queenstown:

> 18869: 'You have told us at the conversation between you and the Chief Engineer the Captain was not present?'
> 'He was not.'
> 18870: 'And that you had no conversation with him during the voyage about speed?'
> 'Absolutely none.'
> 18871: 'Then will you tell us how it was he was to become aware of your decision to increase the speed on the Tuesday?'
> 'I think the Engineer would probably have spoken to him.'
> 18872: 'Did you make any arrangement with the Engineer about that?'
> 'I did not.'
> 18873: 'Then as far as you know the Captain was not aware that you were going to make this increase in speed?'
> 'No.'
> 18874: 'Do you know under whose instructions those extra boilers were put on on a Sunday morning?'

'I do not.'

18875: 'Is that a thing the Chief Engineer would be likely to do on his own account?'

'I should say so.'

18876: 'Unless he had had instructions from the Captain that the speed was to be increased?'

'I think he would if he was going to work up to 78 revolutions.'

18877: 'At all events, you had no conversation with the Captain about it?'

'Absolutely none.'

We also know that Captain Smith handed Ismay the *Baltic* ice warning telegram, which Ismay kept it in his pocket for five hours on the day of *Titanic*'s collision:

18828: 'Now I will come to the question of the *Baltic* telegram. Did you before that particular Sunday know what was the practice with regard to Marconigrams received by the Officers on the ship relating to the navigation of the ship? Did you know what it was the practice to do with those Marconigrams as soon as they had been received?'

'I believe the practice was to put them up in the chart room for the Officers.'

18829: 'Did you know that on Sunday, April the 14th?'

'Yes.'

18830: 'Was not the Marconigram from the *Baltic* essentially a message affecting navigation?'

'Yes.'

18831: 'Then will you say why, under those circumstances, with that knowledge, you put that Marconigram into your pocket?'

'Because it was given to me, as I believe now, just before lunchtime, and I went down and had it in my pocket.'

18832: 'And you suggest that you put it in your pocket simply in a fit of absent-mindedness?'

'Yes, entirely.'

18833: 'And had it occurred to you when you were talking to Mrs. Ryerson that you had absentmindedly put this message into your pocket?'

'It had not.'

18834: 'It had not occurred to you?'

'No.'

18835: 'And you still retained it in your pocket until it was asked for by Captain Smith late in the evening?'

'Ten minutes past seven, I think it was, he asked me for it.'

18836: 'That is to say, it had been in your possession for something like five hours?'

'Yes, I should think so.'

18837: 'And you seriously say it was put into your pocket in a fit of absentmindedness and retained for five hours?'

'Yes.'

18838: 'Although you were discussing it with two of the lady passengers?'

'I was not discussing it with them.'

18839: 'You mentioned it?'
   'I mentioned it.'
18840: 'And took it out and read it?'
   'Yes.'

However, these exchanges are ultimately just examples of Ismay's interest in *Titanic*'s maiden voyage, as owner of the White Star Line, and his close working relationship with his most senior engineer and most senior captain. The reality is that Captain Smith needed no encouragement to go as fast as possible. Although he had both a Managing Director of the shipbuilder and the Chairman of the Line on board for *Titanic*'s maiden voyage, Captain Smith had been in this situation many times before. Indeed, Ismay and Andrews had both been present on the *Olympic*'s maiden voyage, but it was on *Olympic*'s second trip to New York, when neither of them was on board, that *Olympic* arrived early, getting into New York on Tuesday night.

Captain Smith's love of speed comes across clearly in the following passage from Commander Lightoller's memoirs, *Titanic and Other Ships*:

"'Captain Smith, or "E.J." as he was familiarly and affectionately known, was quite a character in the shipping world. Tall, full whiskered, and broad. At first sight you would think to yourself, "Here's a typical Western Ocean Captain." "Bluff, hearty, and I'll bet he's got a voice like a foghorn." As a matter of fact, he had a pleasant, quiet voice and invariable smile. A voice he rarely raised above a conversational tone—

not to say he couldn't; in fact, I have often heard him bark an order that made a man come to himself with a bump. He was a great favourite, and a man any officer would give his ears to sail under.

'I had been with him many years, off and on, in the mail boats, *Majestic*, mainly, and it was an education to see him con his own ship up through the intricate channels entering New York at full speed. One particularly bad corner, known as the South-West Spit, used to make us fairly flush with pride as he swung her round, judging his distances to a nicety; she heeling over to the helm with only a matter of feet to spare between each end of the ship and the banks.'"

This glimpse of Captain Smith's character is added to by the following recollection from his daughter, Helen Melville Smith, which she mentioned on visiting the set of the film *A Night To Remember*, in the late 1950s:

'Cigars were his pleasure. And one was allowed to be in the room only if one was absolutely still, so that the blue cloud over his head never moved.'

Getting into New York early would have suited Smith's quiet flamboyance, so Ismay would not have had to 'order' Smith to do anything. Indeed, Captain Smith came from an era before wireless communication, where all crack transatlantic passenger shipmasters went flat-out in clear weather at all times, trusting only to a good lookout to avoid danger.

21 TITANIC WAS TRYING TO TAKE THE SHORTEST ROUTE TO
NEW YORK AT THE TIME OF THE ACCIDENT.

No. She was, in fact, on the longer route to New York, known
as the southern track, which was agreed to be used by all the
major steamship companies' ships in the summer months
between 15th January and 23rd August. The shorter, winter
route, was known as the northern track. These Atlantic
shipping lanes were established in 1899 with the intention
of avoiding areas where ice and fog was prevalent, keeping
eastbound and westbound ships apart, and increasing the
chances of a ship in distress receiving help from another
vessel travelling on the same route.

However, heavy snowfall in the Arctic in the winter of
1910/11, followed by a warmer than usual Arctic summer in
1911 and a mild winter in 1911/12, resulted in much larger
quantities of ice than usual drifting south in the freezing waters
of the Labrador current, which was flowing faster than usual
that year with high volumes of melt-water from the Arctic.
The customary 'Southern' track was therefore not southern
enough to avoid the ice which *Titanic* encountered.

As a direct result of the *Titanic* disaster, this southern
westbound track was moved further south, with the turning
point known as the 'Corner' moved from 42N, 47W to 39N
45W, 240 miles further southeast, in order to avoid ice more
effectively. Subsequently, the International Convention for
the Safety of Life At Sea was signed on 30th January, 1914.
Amongst other things, this established an international ice
observation and patrol service, which appointed vessels to
patrol the ice regions and provide warnings of icebergs and

derelict wrecks in the major Atlantic shipping lanes. The International Ice Patrol still exists today, and commemorates its origins each year on 15th April, by laying a wreath over *Titanic*'s wreck site.

22 CAPTAIN SMITH SHOULD HAVE SLOWED DOWN FOR ICE.

Yes, but in clear weather, only if he had actually seen ice in his path and determined that it was large enough to cause damage. Prior to the *Titanic* disaster, in clear weather, no transatlantic passenger liner captain ever slowed down for ice until they actually saw it. At the inquiry, captain after captain testified to the fact that they would not, in Smith's position, have slowed down before they saw an iceberg.

Captain Richard Jones, master of the SS *Canada*, Captain Edwin Cannons, master with the Atlantic Transport Company with 25 years' experience in the North Atlantic, Captain John Ranson of White Star Line's *Baltic*, on the Liverpool-New York run, John Pritchard, former captain of Cunard's record-breaking *Mauretania*, and several other captains with long experience of passenger liners and of the Atlantic, all said that it was normal practice to maintain speed even when ice had been reported.

For example, Frederick Passow, who had been a captain on the North Atlantic for 28 years and who had crossed about 700 times, testified:

21891: 'No. If there was any haze the haze would be seen?'

'Immediately. As soon as there is the slightest beard on the green light and we are in the ice region we slow down, because you cannot say how far you can see, but when it is absolutely clear we do not slow down for ice.'

However, Ernest Shackleton, the famous polar explorer, said that he would have slowed down for ice; even in a vessel doing only six knots he would slow down. His was the only dissenting voice, however. His experience with ice was undoubtedly much greater than the liner captains', who all said that it was fairly unusual to find ice so far south in the Atlantic at that time of year. It should also be remembered that in these times before airplanes, competition to achieve fast crossings in all conditions was fierce between the steamship companies, whose passengers demanded speed and consistency. As a liner captain, travelling on the longer, southern route and in seemingly perfect conditions, Smith's decision was a reasonable one, especially given the extraordinary safety record enjoyed by transatlantic passenger liners prior to the *Titanic* disaster, and no other liner captain would have acted differently. It was Smith's misfortune to demonstrate that this common practice was ultimately a flawed one. In his report following the British Inquiry, the Wreck Commissioner, Lord Mersey, concluded:

'It was shown that for many years past, indeed, for a quarter of a century or more, the practice of liners using this track when in the vicinity of ice at night had been in clear weather to keep the course, to maintain the speed and to trust to a sharp look-out to enable them to avoid the danger. This practice, it was said, had been justified by experience, no casualties having resulted from it. I accept the evidence as to the practice and as to the immunity from casualties which is said to have accompanied it. But the event has proved the practice to be bad. Its root is probably to be found in competition and in the desire of the public for quick passages rather than in the judgment of navigators. But unfortunately experience appeared to justify it. In these circumstances I am not able to blame Captain Smith. He had not the experience which his own misfortune has afforded to those whom he has left behind, and he was doing only that which other skilled men would have done in the same position… He made a mistake, a very grievous mistake, but one in which, in face of the practice and of past experience, negligence cannot be said to have had any part; and in the absence of negligence it is, in my opinion, impossible to fix Captain Smith with blame. It is, however, to be hoped that the last has been heard of the practice and that for the future it will be abandoned for what we now know to be more prudent and wiser measures. What was a mistake in the case of the *Titanic* would without doubt be negligence in any similar case in the future.'

23 CRUCIAL ICE WARNINGS NEVER MADE IT TO TITANIC'S BRIDGE BECAUSE THE WIRELESS OPERATOR WAS TOO BUSY AND TIRED.

Probably. The night before *Titanic's* collision, her wireless operators, Jack Phillips and Harold Bride, had spent six hours repairing a damaged transformer in their new Marconi wireless set, with the result that her senior operator, Jack Phillips, was unusually tired at the end of his watch the following day, when the collision occurred. These problems are explained by Harold Bride in the following extract of his 27th April, 1912 report to the Marconi traffic manager, Mr W.R. Cross:

'The night before the disaster Mr. Phillips and myself had had a deal of trouble, owing to the leads from the secondary of the transformer having burnt through inside the casing and make contact with certain iron bolts holding the woodwork and frame together, thereby earthing the power to a great extent. After binding these leads with rubber tape, we once more had the apparatus in perfect working order, but not before we had put in nearly six hours' work, Mr. Phillips being of the opinion that, in the first place, it was the condensers which had broken, and these we had had out and examined before locating the damage in the transformer.

'Owing to this trouble, I had promised to relieve Mr. Phillips on the following night at midnight instead of the usual time, 2 o'clock, as he seemed very tired.'

Even more significantly, shortly before the collision, *Titanic* for the first time came within range of the wireless shore station at Cape Race, approximately 400 miles away. *Titanic's* daytime wireless range was only 400 miles, so this was the first time on the voyage that messages from the ship could now be transmitted direct to land in America, and the tired Jack Phillips was therefore very busy trying to clear this back-log of traffic just prior to the collision.

At 11.45 a.m. on Sunday morning *Titanic* had received a message from the *Amerika* warning of ice south of her track, which was intended for the Hydrographic Office in Washington via Cape Race; this was never delivered to *Titanic's* bridge as it was not intended for her and consequently was not marked for the Master's attention by the MSG (Master Service Gram) prefix. However, since it related to navigation, the operator should have delivered it to the bridge anyway. In the event, it was probably put with the other messages for transmission to Cape Race, once that station came within range. This message did not give the time that *Amerika* had seen the ice.

Far more importantly, at about 9.40pm ship's time, Phillips received a message from the *Mesaba* which may also have lacked the MSG prefix, warning of the icefield into which *Titanic* would shortly collide:

'In Latitude 42N to 41-25N. Long.49 to Long.50-30W. Saw much heavy pack ice, and great number large icebergs. Also field ice. Weather good, clear.'

According to *Titanic's* Second Officer, Charles Herbert

Lightoller, writing more than 20 years later, in his memoirs, *Titanic and other ships*:

> 'The position this ship gave was right ahead of us and not many miles distant. The wireless operator was not to know how close we were to this position, and therefore the extreme urgency of the message. That he received the message is known, and it was read by the other operator in his bunk. The operator who received it was busy at the time, working wireless messages to and from Cape Race, also with his accounts, and he put the message under a paper weight at his elbow, just until he squared up what he was doing, and he would then have brought it to the bridge. **That delay proved fatal and was the main contributory cause to the loss of that magnificent ship and hundreds of lives.**' [Emphasis in author's original.]

Nevertheless, Lightoller was every inch the Company man, and it is not beyond the realms of possibility that this message was in fact delivered to the bridge, and that the bridge did not act upon it, trusting instead to being able to see any ice in time to avoid it, as they had done for years, in clear weather. Indeed, as Lightoller was off duty at the time, and every more senior watch officer died in the disaster, he would not necessarily have known at first hand whether that message had in fact been delivered.

Regardless of which version of events is true, at about 11pm ship's time Phillips received the following message from the *Californian*, the ship nearest to the *Titanic*, only about ten miles away to the northward:

'We are stopped and surrounded by ice'.

This was only moments before *Titanic* collided with an outlying berg in the same north/south-running ice barrier which had brought *Californian* to a stop.

However, *Californian*'s wireless operator, Cyril Evans, had not followed the usual etiquette among wireless operators of waiting until Phillips had finished communicating with Cape Race. This was probably because Evans wanted to go to sleep after 16 hours on watch and *Titanic*'s communications with Cape Race would have been fast and incessant. When Evans interrupted Phillips, the loud spark from the *Californian*, lying only about 10 miles to the northward of *Titanic*, blasted in Phillips' ears as he was listening to the much quieter signals from Cape Race, 400 miles away. This painful interruption would have obliterated the communication Phillips was sending, meaning he would have to begin his current sentence again. Phillips instinctively told *Californian* to 'Shut up' or 'Keep out', and explained: 'I am working Cape Race.' This was not unusual in the Marconi banter of the day, and would not have been taken as a great insult, but in his haste and pique, Phillips did not ask for Evans's position and did not inform the bridge of this communication.

Now that Evans, *Californian*'s only radio operator, had now communicated with the only ship within wireless range of the *Californian*, as he had been ordered to do by Captain Lord, he switched off his wireless apparatus and went to bed, ending his long day on watch. For this reason, *Californian* did not hear *Titanic*'s distress signal, transmitted an hour and a half later.

In 1912, wireless technology was still in its infancy and experienced captains tended to rely on a sharp lookout, as they had always done, regarding wireless as a useful but inessential novelty. Many ships still did not have wireless and many of those that did, such as the *Californian* and *Carpathia*, only had one operator, meaning that messages were dependent on the wireless operator being awake and on watch. There was no way of taking messages to the bridge other than having the operator physically take it, which would then take them away from the set. There was provision for a messenger boy, but Bride said having one was more trouble than it was worth, with the result that there wasn't one on the *Titanic*.

Many of the problems stemmed from the fact that wireless operators were employed by the wireless company, in *Titanic*'s case the Marconi Co., rather than by the White Star Line. They were therefore primarily on the ship to send passenger messages commercially on behalf of their employer, although they were supposed to prioritise government and navigational messages. Most Marconi operators were young men who loved the new technology, but they were very poorly paid and often overworked. The backlog caused by the earlier breakdown of the wireless set meant that Titanic's Marconi operators were busier than ever. Bride was planning to relieve Phillips two hours early because he was so exhausted from repairing the equipment and trying to keep up with the traffic—and Phillips was lucky to have a relief. Harold Cottam, the sole Marconi operator on the rescue ship *Carpathia*, only picked up *Titanic*'s distress signal as he was bending down to untie his boots and go to bed! Cottam was later completely overwhelmed with trying to deal with the huge volume of messages concerning the sinking, and *Titanic's* rescued junior operator, Harold Bride, had to be dragged off his sick bed, where he was suffering from severely frost-bitten feet, to assist Cottam.

Had there been two operators on the *Californian*, she would have picked up *Titanic's* distress signal immediately; 24 hour radio watch for ships was therefore one of the most important pieces of safety regulation brought in as a result of the *Titanic* disaster.

24 CAPTAIN SMITH WAS DRUNK AT THE TIME OF THE COLLISION.

No. Although it is true that Captain Smith had attended a dinner party earlier that evening held in his honour by the Wideners, he never drank whilst at sea, and this party was no exception, as Mrs Widener's affidavit at the US Inquiry confirmed:

> STATE OF PENNSYLVANIA, County of Philadelphia, ss *Titanic*:
>
> Mrs. George D. Widener, being duly sworn according to law, deposes and says as follows:

'I was a passenger with my husband, George D. Widener, and my son, Harry Widener, on the steamship *Titanic* of the White Star Line on her voyage from Southampton on the 10th day of April, 1912. On the night of Sunday, the 14th of April, 1912, my husband and I gave a dinner at which Capt. Smith was present. Capt. Smith drank absolutely no wine or intoxicating liquor of any kind whatever at the dinner.'

ELEANOR ELKINS WIDENER

Sworn to and subscribed before me this 29th day of May, 1912.

This evidence is corroborated by the testimony of Charles E. Stengel, at the US Inquiry:

CES111: (Senator Smith) 'Was there any evidence of intoxication among the officers or crew that night?'
'No, sir. I have a distinct recollection of a Mrs. Thorne stating, while talking about the captain being to dinner, that she was in that party, and she said, "I was in that party, and the captain did not drink a drop." He smoked two cigars, that was all, and left the dining room about 10 o'clock.'

In fact, we know from Lightoller's testimony, which is corroborated by Boxhall's, that Captain Smith returned to the bridge at about five minutes to nine.

Passengers

25 'MOLLY' BROWN WAS TREATED WITH CONDESCENSION BY OTHER FIRST CLASS PASSENGERS BECAUSE SHE WAS 'NEW MONEY'.

No. James Cameron's 1997 film gave the impression that the majority of First Class passengers were boring and narrow-minded snobs who were disdainful of Mrs Brown's liveliness and status as a nouveau riche. The film of *A Night to Remember* also shows a vivid contrast between the vulgarity of 'Molly' and the more subdued presentation of First Class 'grandees'. In fact, this portrayal does a great disservice both to her fellow passengers and 'Molly'. Although Margaret Brown was undoubtedly nouveau riche, her fortune coming from her husband's recent success in gold mining, she was no more out of place than a number of other passengers whose fortune was new. These included Isidor Straus, a German Jewish immigrant who had worked his way up from a general store to co-found Macy's department store with his brother; and Charles Hays, President of the Grand Trunk Railway, who was educated at American state-funded schools and began working as a clerk in the passenger department of the Pacific and Atlantic Railroad at the age of 17.

In fact, Mrs Brown had spent the winter with Col. John Jacob Astor and his pregnant wife Madeleine, in Egypt, before returning home with them on the *Titanic*. The Astors were one of the oldest and richest families in America, but the Colonel's sudden divorce and re-marriage had shocked Edwardian society. No doubt there was some snobbishness, but the contrast between Mrs Brown and her fellow passengers as one of new versus old money is a simplistic one. In reality, Margaret Brown was well-connected and well-educated, and not at all the coarse and illiterate character portrayed by the films and by the 1960s Broadway musical *The Unsinkable Molly Brown*, which christened her 'Molly'—a name she never used—because it was thought more catchy and easier to sing. The epithet of 'unsinkable' came from her own words to reporters after the disaster:

'The ship can sink, but I can't; I'm unsinkable!'

The child of Irish immigrants like her husband, in 1901 the 34-year-old Margaret Brown was one of the first students to enroll at the Carnegie Institute in New York, where she studied languages and literature. She spoke French, Russian, and German, and her linguistic skills proved an asset for communicating with immigrants who spoke no English on board the *Carpathia*, where she also established the Survivors' Committee and helped to raise $10,000 for those left destitute by the shipwreck, before the *Carpathia* had even reached New York! She did not leave the ship until she had ensured all the survivors had somewhere to go. A month or so later she presented a silver cup to Captain Rostron and medals to his crew as thanks for their outstanding work in rescuing the *Titanic*'s survivors.

Margaret was also notable for her lifelong advocacy of women's and labour rights, literacy and education, and used her post-*Titanic* fame, combined with her fortune, to speak out about these issues. She was one of the first women in America to run for political office, helped by living in Colorado, where women had had the vote since 1893. She also chaired an international conference on women's rights in 1914. In 1932 she was awarded the French Legion d'Honneur for her 'good citizenship', including her ongoing work on behalf of *Titanic* survivors and her relief work during the First World War.

26 ALICE CLEAVER, NURSEMAID TO A FAMILY IN FIRST CLASS, HAD PREVIOUSLY BEEN CONVICTED OF KILLING HER OWN CHILD.

No. However, due to an unfortunate coincidence of names, this story has persisted, probably partly because of its connection with the sad story of the Allison family, whose daughter, Helen Loraine Allison, was the only child on *Titanic* in either First or Second class to be lost.

The *Titanic* passenger and Allison family nursemaid was Alice Catherine Cleaver, who apparently led an otherwise blameless life, going on to marry and have children of her own after the *Titanic* disaster. But Alice Mary Cleaver, who was not on the *Titanic* and had no connection with Alice Catherine Cleaver, other than their shared Christian and surnames, was convicted of murder in 1909 for throwing her baby under a train. Her sentence was commuted from

67

the death penalty to imprisonment, as was common in such cases, before the crime of infanticide was defined as a separate offence by the Infanticide Act of 1922. Alice Mary Cleaver died of tuberculosis in 1915.

There is some mystery as to exactly what happened on *Titanic* regarding the nursemaid Alice Catherine Cleaver and the Allison family. She has sometimes been blamed for her actions in taking the Allisons' son, Trevor, away in a lifeboat without letting the rest of the Allison family know, thereby causing them to keep looking for Trevor unnecessarily. This resulted in the death of the rest of the family, including their other child, Loraine. One version is that she helped Mrs Bess Allison to dress and tried to persuade her to come on deck, but Bess became hysterical and wouldn't go. Alice then took her charge, Trevor (it seems she was appointed to look after Trevor only, because he had been ill), and went into Second Class to round up the rest of the family's servants, before entering a lifeboat with Trevor. No-one will ever know exactly what happened, but Major Peuchen, who knew the family, said that Bess had got out of her lifeboat with Loraine after being told that her husband was boarding a boat on the other side of the ship. When she got there, Mr Allison was nowhere in sight, and meanwhile the boat she had been in was gone. There are several conflicting reports, however. Major Peuchen also thought that she was 'hustled into one of the collapsible lifeboats' when she failed to find her husband, and that she was last seen 'toppling out of the half-swamped boat' (probably Collapsible A, although Peuchen had left *Titanic* earlier in the evening in lifeboat Number 6). Nursemaid Alice Cleaver did not realise until the next day that the rest of the Allison family had not survived, and its likely she simply acted to make sure Trevor was safe, assuming that the Allisons knew where Trevor was and that Mr Allison would look after his wife and Loraine. A report in the press after the disaster said that the Allisons were last seen on the promenade deck, smiling.

27 TWO KIDNAPPED CHILDREN SURVIVED THE SINKING OF THE TITANIC.

Yes. The Navratil brothers, Michel Marcel aged three and Edmond Roger aged two, had been taken by their father in a custody kidnapping. Michel Navratil Sr, who was originally from Slovakia but at this time was living in Nice, France, had married an Italian woman, Marcelle Caretto, in 1907 but he separated from her in 1912 over business difficulties and an alleged affair on Marcelle's part. Marcelle had custody of the children, but Michel kidnapped them during a visit at Easter, planning to take them to America. He travelled to England from France via Monte Carlo, and boarded the *Titanic* at Southampton.

On board he pretended to be a widower under the name of his friend Louis Hoffmann and kept the boys close, although he once allowed a Swiss passenger, Bertha Lehmann, to look after them while he played a game of cards.

As the *Titanic* was sinking, Michel and another passenger dressed the boys and took them up on deck, where they were put on board Collapsible D, the last boat to be properly launched. Michel Sr was lost in the sinking.

Michel Jr and Edmond spoke no English, so survivor Margaret Hays, who was fluent in French and had looked after them on the *Carpathia*, took the boys into her New York home until their relatives could be found. Eventually Marcelle, recognising her sons from newspaper photographs, was brought over to New York by the White Star Line and reunited with them on May 16 1912. The reunited mother and children then sailed back to Europe together on the *Oceanic*.

28 THERE WERE PROFESSIONAL 'CARD-SHARPS' TRAVELLING ON TITANIC AS FIRST CLASS PASSENGERS.

Yes. Although the famous 'Jay Yates', who was allegedly travelling under the name of J.H. Rogers and was hailed as a 'hero' who helped women and children into the lifeboats, was never actually on board. As featured in the film version of Walter Lord's *A Night To Remember*, he was believed to have given the following message to a woman getting into a boat:

> 'If saved, inform my sister, Mrs. J. F. Adams of Findlay, Ohio. Lost
> [Signed] J. H. Rogers.'

In fact, Yates was a con man and gambler who was wanted by the police. He used the *Titanic* story to fake his own death in order to escape detection, but he was later arrested while using another alias.

However, there were at least three professional gamblers

who were on board and travelling under assumed names, including Charles H. Romaine, who on *Titanic*'s maiden voyage travelled under the name C. Rolmane. He was rescued, probably in lifeboat number 15, along with notorious gambler George (Boy) Brereton, travelling as George Brayton, who was likewise attempting to draw unsuspecting passengers into dishonest card games. Harry Haven (Kid) Homer, another gambler, also survived the disaster; he was travelling aboard *Titanic* under the name H. Haven.

A man named Alvin Thompson was sometimes said to have been on board because of his nickname of '*Titanic* Thompson', but he had no connection to the ship and it seems this name was given to him subsequently for his role in several gambling disasters.

The White Star Line were fully aware that professional gamblers frequented trans-Atlantic ocean liners and included the following mild warning with *Titanic*'s maiden voyage passenger list:

SPECIAL NOTICE

The attention of the Managers has been called to the fact that certain persons, believed to be Professional Gamblers, are in the habit of travelling to and fro in Atlantic Steamships.

In bringing this to the knowledge of Travelers the Managers, while not wishing in the slightest degree to interfere with the freedom of action of Patrons of the White Star Line, desire to invite their assistance in discouraging Games of Chance, as being likely to afford these individuals special opportunities for taking unfair advantage of others.

29 STEWARDESS VIOLET JESSOP SURVIVED THE SINKING OF BOTH THE TITANIC AND HER SISTER SHIP, THE BRITANNIC.

Yes. Violet Jessop was lucky throughout her life! Having survived tuberculosis as a child, she became a stewardess to help support her family after the death of her father, and served on all three *Olympic* Class ships. She was on board the *Olympic* during the collision with HMS *Hawke*; she then transferred to the *Titanic*, from which she escaped in lifeboat Number 16. She then served as a Voluntary Aid Detachment nurse during the First World War on *Titanic's* slightly younger sister, HMHS *Britannic*, which had been requisitioned as a hospital ship and was sunk in 1916 in the Aegean, off Cape Sounion.

Jessop escaped in one of the last lifeboats to leave the ship, only to be sucked into *Britannic's* giant propellers, as her Captain was still trying to reach shallow water to beach the ship. Whilst under water, Jessop suffered repeated blows to her head, as she passed under one of *Britannic's* propellers. By pure chance she survived and came to the surface surrounded by severed corpses and grotesquely injured men. Years later, Violet discovered that she had in fact suffered a fractured skull at the time, though she assumed for months afterwards that it was nothing more than bad headaches. Violet, who was a strikingly attractive young woman, concluded that it must have been her very thick hair which saved her!

30 ALL EIGHT MEMBERS OF THE GOODWIN FAMILY DIED IN THE SINKING.

Yes. Frederick Goodwin was a 42-year-old electrical engineer living in a terraced house in Fulham, England, with his wife, Augusta, 43 and six children, Lillian, 16; Charles, 14; William, 11; Jessie, 10; Harold, 9; and baby Sidney Leslie Goodwin, born on 9th September, 1910, and therefore about 18 months' old.

Frederick's brother, Thomas, who had settled in Niagra Falls, New York, notified him of an opening at a large power station there, so Frederick decided to move to America with his family. Selling their home in Fulham, they paused briefly in Marcham, booking passage on a small steamer operating out of Southampton. With few savings, they were travelling Third Class but their sailing was cancelled due to the coal strike and they were transferred to the *Titanic*.

The entire family was lost in the sinking.

One of the first bodies recovered by the cable ship Mackay-Bennett was that of a small, fair haired boy:

NO. 4—MALE—ESTIMATED AGE, 2—HAIR, FAIR
CLOTHING—Grey coat with fur on collar and cuffs; brown serge frock; petticoat; flannel garment; pink woolen singlet—brown shoes and stockings.
NO MARKS WHATEVER
PROBABLY THIRD CLASS

The sailors who recovered this body were so moved that when

no relative came forward to claim the child, they personally escorted the coffin to Fairview Lawn Cemetery in Halifax and paid for a large monument in memory of the 'unknown child'. His was the only burial service that day—4th May, 1912—and they buried him with a copper pendant marked 'Our Babe'. In 2002 the body previously identified only as 'the unknown child' was identified as Eino Viljami Panula by means of DNA technology, but in 2007 the researchers revised their opinion following further analysis of the DNA and stated that the body was in fact that of Sidney Leslie Goodwin.

'Iceberg, right ahead!'

31 'KEEP A LOOKOUT FOR SMALL ICE' WAS A STANDING JOKE AMONGST TITANIC'S LOOKOUTS.

Yes. It is interesting to note that earlier Lightoller had ordered that the Crow's Nest be telephoned a second time to ensure they understood specifically to 'keep a sharp lookout for small ice *and growlers*'. This was almost certainly because he knew that the first part of this order was a standing joke among lookout men, which they regularly passed to one another at the change of watch, regardless of their ship's location or the weather conditions, as lookout George Hogg revealed at the British inquiry:

> 17537: 'You did hear it at 6 o'clock, "Keep a look-out for small ice"?'
> 'Yes, but I believe it is the usual password in the nests in these ships.'
> 17538: 'I do not understand what you mean by that?'
> 'I do not believe they got it from the bridge at the time.'
> 17539: 'Never mind where they got it from. You got it from them?'
> 'Yes.'
> 17540: 'Who gave it to you?'

'Fleet and Lee—I think Lee gave it to me.'

17541: 'You say you believe it is a usual password. Had you ever had it given you before, a password of that kind?'

'Sometimes.'

17542: 'But I mean on this voyage?'

'Yes. I believe I did: I would not be quite sure. It seems a password there from what I can see of it.'

17543: (The Commissioner.) 'I do not understand what you mean by a "password." What do you mean?'

'A joke, Sir. I should think.'

17544: (The Attorney-General.) 'A joke to the look-out men to keep a look-out for ice?'

'This is what is passed on to one another.'

17545: 'Have you any recollection of their doing that to you on that night at 6 o'clock in the evening?'

'At 6 o'clock in the evening: "Nothing doing; keep a look-out for small ice."'

17546: (The Commissioner.) 'I am not sure that I understand you when you say you regarded that as a joke. What do you mean?'

'Well, as I say, it seems a password.'

17547: 'Do you mean by "a password" a mere matter of form?'

'That is what they always seemed to say to me, Sir.'

17548: 'What?'

'"Keep a look-out for ice" as we relieved each other.'

17551: (The Attorney-General.) 'How often had you heard it, if at all, before 6 o'clock that evening?'

'I heard it several times before that.'

17554: 'Several days before?'

'We were only out about three days.'

17555: 'I know.'

'A couple of days before.'

17556: 'Do you mean that every time you went and relieved them they gave you that password, as you call it?'

'Yes.'

17557: 'Daytime or nighttime?'

'Any time they would pass it along to one another.'

32 TITANIC'S LOOKOUTS COULD SMELL THE ICE THAT NIGHT.

Yes. The reference in James Cameron's 1997 film, *Titanic*, to lookout Reginald Lee's claim that he could 'smell ice' stems from Lee's testimony at the British inquiry:

2662: 'You knew that ice was about?'

'You could smell it.'

The Commissioner:

'Smell it?'

Mr. Harbinson:

'That is his reply.'

In fact George Symons, on the lookout with Archie Jewell, before Fleet and Lee, testified that he could smell the ice as early as 9 p.m.:

> 11334: 'You know Sunday, the night of the 14th April; do you remember getting special orders from the bridge?'
>
> 'Yes; we had special orders about 9.30.'
>
> 11335: '9.30 that night?'
>
> 'Yes.'
>
> 11336: 'Through the telephone?'
>
> 'Through the telephone.'
>
> 11337: 'Do you know from whom?'
>
> 'No, I could not say.'
>
> 11338: 'From some Officer on the bridge?'
>
> 'From some Officer on the bridge.'
>
> 11339: 'Can you tell me what he said?'
>
> '"Keep a sharp look-out for small ice and bergs till daylight, and pass the word along." That was the order received by Jewell and me; we both heard it through the phone.'
>
> 11340: 'Had you noticed anything to lead you to think you might meet icebergs before you got that message?'
>
> 'Yes; just a small conversation, I think, about 9 o'clock. My mate turned round from time to time and said, "It is very cold here." I said, "Yes; by the smell of it there is ice about." He asked me why, and I said, "As a Rule you can smell the ice before you get to it."'

First Class passenger Elizabeth Weed Shutes also smelt the ice before the collision that night and described it in the opening paragraph of her 1912 account, *When the Titanic went down*, as follows:

> 'Such a biting cold air poured into my stateroom that I could not sleep, and the air had so strange an odor, as if it came from a clammy cave. I had noticed that same odor in the ice cave on the Eiger glacier.'

Lookouts Lee and Symons were referring to that same smell of ice which Elizabeth Shutes noticed. Unfortunately, being able to smell the ice surrounding *Titanic* that night did not save the ship, since it was quite normal to be close enough to ice to smell it in the freezing waters of the Labrador Current, but still be able to see an iceberg in time to avoid it.

33 IF TITANIC'S LOOKOUTS HAD HAD BINOCULARS, THEY'D HAVE SEEN THE ICEBERG EARLIER.

No. Binoculars are intended for inspecting objects which have first been picked up by the naked eye. Using them to search for objects actually makes those objects harder to find as they dramatically restrict the field of vision; at sea they are also much less clear than the naked eye. One should also remember that it was pitch dark, and that binocular technology at the turn of the century was not very advanced. George Bartlett, Marine Superintendent of the White Star

Line and Commander in the Royal Naval Reserve with 30 years' experience at sea, 18 of which were on the Atlantic, said at the British Inquiry that in his experience binoculars were of use to officers, but not to seamen. It was the lookout's job to simply notify the bridge immediately of anything they had seen, and the bridge would then use binoculars to identify the object:

> 21713: 'look-out men are there to use their eyes and to report immediately anything they see, not to find out the character of that object they see.'

Bartlett thought that there should never be binoculars in the crow's nest as it might encourage the look-outs to find out what they had seen, which was not their job and which would only delay them. Their job was to immediately ring the bell the moment they saw anything.

Others, including Bertram Hayes, master of another White Star Line vessel, agreed with this view. Second Officer Charles Lightoller thought that binoculars might be useful if a light had been seen at a distance, in which case the officers might ring to ask the lookout to identify it. However, he agreed that in the case of a 'derelict wreck or iceberg', the lookout should immediately alert the bridge by striking the bell before making any attempt to identify what he had seen:

> 14293: 'If one of those men on the look-out had seen something and applied the glasses is it not possible that he might have been able to identify it as an iceberg

sooner than with the naked eye?'

'He might be able to identify it, but we do not wish him to identify it. All we want him to do is to strike the bells.'

14294: 'I will put this to you: Supposing a man on the look-out fancies he sees something and strikes the bell, and it turns out not to be anything, I should think he would be reprimanded?'

'He is in every case commended.'

The policy on whether glasses should be supplied to the crow's-nest was set by the captain, and Titanic therefore was not obliged to supply them to the lookout men. Captain Lord of the *Californian* also considered the provision of glasses to lookouts unnecessary, and had only once done so, on the morning of April 15th, 1912, when he sent a lookout up above the crow's nest to look for *Titanic*:

STL121: 'Would glasses in the hands of the lookout be of any assistance in determining proximity to ice?'

'No, I should not think so. I would never think of giving a man in the lookout a pair of glasses.'

STL122: 'And have never done so?'

'I did once. I do not think I will ever again.'

STL123: 'When did you do it?'

'The morning I was looking for the *Titanic*, I gave a pair to the lookout. I pulled a man up to the main truck in a coal basket when I heard of it, so he would have a good view around, and gave him a pair of glasses.'

STL124: 'Let us understand each other. That was at the time when you were increasing your vigilance?'

'Yes, sir.'

STL125: 'And when you had sent an additional lookout to the crow's nest?'

'No; I pulled him up to the main truck, which is about 30 feet higher than the crow's nest; pulled him up in a coal basket.'

STL126: 'When you did that, you gave him glasses?'

'Gave him glasses.'

STL127: 'Of course, that was in daylight?'

'Oh, yes.'

STL128: 'And that is the only time you ever used glasses in the crow's nest?'

'The first time I ever heard of it.'

STL129: 'Let me ask, where did you get these glasses that you gave to that extra lookout that morning?'

'I took them off the bridge; a spare pair that were on the bridge.'

STL130: 'You have glasses on the bridge for your own use?'

'Yes.'

STL131: 'And yet you have no glasses in the crow's nest for the use of the lookout?'

'No.'

34 TITANIC WAS GOING AT THE MAXIMUM SPEED SHE WAS
CAPABLE OF WHEN SHE SIGHTED THE ICEBERG.

Not quite. Although *Titanic*'s engine telegraph was set to
'full speed ahead' at the time, and the ship was going faster
than at any other time during her maiden voyage, *Titanic*
had nevertheless not yet reached the maximum speed she was
capable of. Quartermaster Robert Hichens testified that in
the two hours between 8 p.m. and 10 p.m. on the evening of
14th April *Titanic* covered 45 nautical miles, thus averaging
22.5 knots. This was not her top speed, as Ismay testified:

> JBI014: 'I understand it has been stated that the ship
> was going at full speed. The ship never had been at
> full speed. The full speed of the ship is 78 revolutions.
> She works up to 80. So far as I am aware, she never
> exceeded 75 revolutions. She had not all her boilers
> on. None of the single-ended boilers were on.'

Third Officer Herbert Pitman, based on his own knowledge
that she was doing 75 revolutions, estimated *Titanic*'s speed
that evening to be over 21 knots, but informed the British
Enquiry that this was nothing compared to what they
expected her to achieve:

> HJP272. 'And at that time the speed of the ship was
> about 21+ knots per hour?'
>   'Yes, sir.'
> HJP273: 'Did you regard that as pretty good speed?'
>   'No; nothing to what we expected her to do.'

HJP274: 'Did you expect her to do pretty well?'
'We thought it quite possible that she could reach 24.'

Pitman's estimate of 24 knots is corroborated by the following deposition given for the *Titanic* Limited Liability Hearings in 1913, by Edward Wilding, one of the ship's designers, who was on board *Titanic* on her run from her trials in Belfast to Southampton:

'During April 3rd when running south, we obtained a speed of about 23.25 knots for several hours.'

Based on this performace, almost before her engines had settled in at all, *Titanic* would probably have easily achieved 24 knots per hour at some point during the following day, once all her boilers had been connected up and she had had a chance to work up her engine revolutions in the calm conditions that were prevailing on her maiden voyage, but she never had the chance. In a poignant reminder of *Titanic*'s short life, White Star Line Chairman J. Bruce Ismay said at the American inquiry:

'It was our intention, if we had fine weather on Monday afternoon or Tuesday, to drive the ship at full speed. That, owing to the unfortunate catastrophe, never eventuated.'

35 TITANIC'S ENGINES WERE PUT IN REVERSE JUST BEFORE THE
COLLISION, MAKING THE SHIP LESS RESPONSIVE TO HER HELM
AND COMPOUNDING THE ACCIDENT.

No. The only evidence we have of *Titanic*'s engines being
put in reverse comes from Fourth officer Boxhall, who did
not arrive on *Titanic*'s bridge until immediately after the
collision.

It is most likely that the order Murdoch rang down to the
engine room was simply 'stop', which would have no adverse
effect of *Titanic*'s ability to turn. This order was indicated in
the boiler rooms by a red light.

We know this from the following testimony given by
Leading Fireman Fred Barratt to Senator Smith in one of
Olympic's boiler rooms, whilst she was berthed in New York.
It is interesting to note that even this order was not received
in time to fully act upon it before the collision:

FRB006: 'Were you there when the accident
occurred?'
'Yes. I was standing talking to the second engineer.
The bell rang, the red light showed. We sang out "shut
the doors" (indicating the ash doors to the furnaces)
and there was a crash just as we sung out. The water
came through the ship's side.'

Titanic therefore had no time to reduce her speed prior to
the collision, meaning her turning ability was not adversely
affected in any way.

36 IF TITANIC HAD BEEN GOING MORE SLOWLY, SHE COULD HAVE TURNED MORE QUICKLY.

No. If *Titanic* had been travelling more slowly, she would also have turned more slowly. Edward Wilding, one of *Titanic*'s designers, explained this at the British inquiry. Wilding had carried out tests on *Titanic*'s sister ship, the *Olympic*, and recorded that:

> '...whereas in 37 seconds you turn two points at the higher speed, in 74 seconds at the lower speed you will not turn very much more than the two points; that is to say, the turning circle is about the same at the two speeds, but that at the slower speed it takes double as long as at the other. Therefore, you do not by decreasing your speed affect very much your power of averting that which it is your object to avert by your action.'

Nevertheless, if *Titanic* had been travelling more slowly the lookouts would have had more time to react to their sighting of the iceberg and been able to give a warning at a greater distance from it, which might have made enough difference to avoid a collision.

Furthermore, travelling at half the speed, *Titanic* would have collided with the iceberg with only a quarter of the force, and this would probably have opened up fewer watertight compartments, and resulted in *Titanic* staying afloat, although she would still have been badly damaged.

37 TITANIC'S RUDDER WAS TOO SMALL FOR HER SIZE, MAKING
HER HARD TO TURN.

No. In fact *Titanic* turned very well. Her stern easily cleared
the iceberg under port helm, when she had—only moments
before—been under full starboard helm, which had succeeded
in throwing her stem clear of the iceberg. Travelling at about
22 knots and seeing the iceberg at only about 500 yards,
Titanic had no more than about 30 seconds in which to avoid
the ice. During this time, she managed to turn two points to
port, before then swinging her bow to starboard, successfully
clearing her stern away from the deadly iceberg.

It is important to note that *Titanic* had exactly the
same size rudder as the *Olympic* had throughout her career,
and *Olympic*'s wartime captain described her as the most
maneuverable and responsive ship he had ever had the
pleasure to command. The very efficient steering of the
Olympic-class liners was due to the advantage that their
central propellors were directly in front of the rudder,
which therefore increased the rudder's effectiveness due to
the increased slipstream produced by the central propellor
(a feature lacking in Cunard's quadruple-screw *Mauretania*
and *Lusitania*). *Olympic*'s captain was even able to suddenly
and deliberately steer into an enemy submarine, ramming
and sinking it and thereby giving *Olympic* the distinction of
being the only merchant ship to sink an enemy vessel during
the First World War.

38 HARD-A-STARBOARD WAS THE ONLY HELM ORDER GIVEN TO AVOID THE ICEBERG.

No. Hard-a-starboard was the first order given, but this was immediately followed by the opposite order, 'Hard-a-port'. This was a standard manoeuvre called 'porting about'. In 1912, helm orders were still based on the old sailing-ship tiller movements, so hard-a-starboard meant 'put the tiller to starboard (right)', thus turning the rudder, and therefore the ship, to port (left). The first part of First Officer Murdoch's order therefore swung *Titanic*'s bow to port (left), but this order alone would have presented her entire starboard side to the iceberg, all the way along to her starboard propeller. The damage caused by this could have caused *Titanic* to capsize and sink within minutes. The second part of the order, 'Hard-a-port' was therefore intended to swing the ship's bow back towards the iceberg, in order to swing her stern clear. Murdoch's second order, 'Hard-a-port', did succeed in swinging *Titanic*'s stern clear of the berg, but the first order, 'hard-a-starboard', had not been given early enough to avoid a collision with the bluff of her bow. This late avoiding action may also have been compounded by the *Titanic*'s running over an underwater ice shelf at the base of the iceberg, caused by erosion and melting of the upper part of the iceberg in the warm waters of the Gulf Stream, which overran the much cooler waters of the Labrador Current in that part of the Atlantic. This may explain why a number of witnesses also described a scraping along the bottom of *Titanic* at the time of her collision.

Quartermaster Alfred Olliver, who was just entering the

bridge as the collision occurred, only heard the second part of this porting about manoeuvre, 'Hard-a-port!':

ALO021: 'Do you know whether the wheel was hard aport then?'

'What I know about the wheel—I was stand-by to run messages, but what I knew about the helm is, hard aport.'

ALO022: 'Do you mean hard aport or hard astarboard?'

'I know the orders I heard when I was on the bridge was after we had struck the iceberg. I heard hard aport, and there was the man at the wheel and the officer. The officer was seeing it was carried out right.'

ALO023: 'What officer was it?'

'Mr. Moody, the sixth officer, was stationed in the wheelhouse.'

ALO024: 'Who was the man at the wheel?'

'Hichens, quartermaster.'

ALO025: 'You do not know whether the helm was put hard astarboard first, or not?'

'No, sir; I do not know that.'

ALO026: 'But you know it was put hard aport after you got there?'

'After I got there; yes, sir.'

ALO027: 'Where was the iceberg, do you think, when the helm was shifted?'

'The iceberg was away up stern.'

ALO028: 'That is when the order "hard aport" was given?'

'That is when the order "hard aport" was given; yes, sir.'

ALO029: 'Who gave the order?'

'The first officer.'

That *Titanic* was thus turned to starboard immediately after she turned to port is also confirmed by Fourth Officer Joseph Boxhall, fireman Alfred Shiers and Able Seaman Joseph Scarrott, all of whom saw the iceberg off *Titanic*'s starboard quarter immediately following the collision, as Scarrott explained to the British Inquiry:

350: 'When you got on deck did you see anything; did you see any ice or iceberg?'

'Oh, yes, when we first came up.'

351: 'Tell me what you saw?'

'When we came up [immediately after the collision], that was before the boatswain's call, we saw a large quantity of ice on the starboard side on the fore-well deck, and I went and looked over the rail there and I saw an iceberg that I took it we had struck. It would be abaft the beam then—abaft the starboard beam.'

352: 'Was it close to?'

'No, it seemed the ship was acting on her helm and we had swung clear of the iceberg.'

353: 'But how far away from your beam was the iceberg, a ship's length or two ships' length?'

'Not a ship's length.'

354: 'You speak of this ship as if answering her helm—

as if answering under which helm?'

355: 'Under port helm. Her stern was slewing off the iceberg. Her starboard quarter was going off the iceberg, and the starboard bow was going as if to make a circle round it.'

356: 'She was acting as if under port helm, her head going to starboard?'

'That is correct.'

359: (Mr. Butler Aspinall) 'Yes.' (To the Witness.) 'You have told us that somewhere on your starboard beam, within a ship's length of you, was the iceberg. How high was the iceberg as compared with your vessel?'

'I should say about as high as the boat deck; it appeared to be that from the position of it.'

360: (The Commissioner) 'How high from the water would that be—90 feet?'

'I cannot say.'

The Attorney-General:

'I think about 60 feet.'

361: (Mr. Butler Aspinall) 'What was the shape of this iceberg?'

'Well, it struck me at the time that it resembled the Rock of Gibraltar looking at it from Europa Point. It looked very much the same shape as that, only much smaller.'

362: (The Commissioner) 'Like a lion couchant?'

'As you approach Gibraltar—it seemed that shape. The highest point would be on my right, as it appeared to me.'

Had *Titanic* only turned hard-a-starboard, as is popularly believed, the iceberg would instead have been off *Titanic*'s port quarter after the collision.

And Quartermaster Rowe, standing at the stern of the ship, noted that the iceberg didn't hit *Titanic*'s propellers, which he testified would have happened had *Titanic*'s helm been hard-a starboard as she passed the iceberg:

> GTR083: 'Do you think the propeller hit the ice? Did you feel any jolt like the propeller hitting the ice?'
> 'No, sir.'
> GTR084: 'Do you not think the propeller would have hit the ice if the helm had been turned hard a starboard?'
> 'Yes, sir.'

This manoeuvre, ending with 'Hard-a-port', meant that *Titanic*, which had been heading west towards New York, ended up heading northwards (towards where the *Californian* had stopped for the night), as also testified by Quartermaster Rowe:

> 17669: 'Was your vessel's head swinging at the time you saw this light of this other vessel?'
> 'I put it down that her stern was swinging.'
> 17670: 'Which way was her stern swinging?'
> 'Practically dead south, I believe, then.'
> 17671: 'Do you mean her head was facing south?'
> 'No, her head was facing north. She was coming round to starboard.'

17672: 'The stern was swung to the south?'
'Yes.'
17673: 'And at that time you saw this white light?'
'Yes.'
17674: 'How was it bearing from you?'
'When I first saw it it was half a point on the port bow, and roughly about two points when I left the bridge.'

39 CAPTAIN SMITH WAS IN BED WHEN TITANIC COLLIDED WITH THE ICEBERG.

No. Captain Smith excused himself from the Wideners' dinner party, where he did not drink, at about 8.45 p.m., and went straight up to *Titanic's* bridge, where he arrived at 8.55 p.m. and continued talking with Second Officer Lightoller until 9.25 p.m., when he left the bridge, saying, 'If it becomes at all doubtful let me know at once; I will be just inside.' But Boxhall, on watch from 8pm until midnight, observed Captain Smith on and around the bridge continually from 9 p.m. until the time of the collision at 11.40 p.m.:

GB317: 'Did you see the captain frequently Sunday night?'
'I saw him frequently during the watch, sir.'
JGB318: 'During the watch?'
'Yes, sir.'
JGB319: 'From 8 o'clock on?'

'Up to the time of the accident.'

JGB320: 'Up to the time the *Titanic* sank?'

'Yes, sir.'

JGB321: 'How frequently?'

'On and off, most of the watch.'

JGB322: 'Where was he when you saw him at these times?'

'Sometimes out on the outer bridge. I would go out and report. I was working observations out, if you understand, most of that watch working out different calculations and reporting to him; and that is how it was I came in contact with him so much.'

JGB323: 'Where was he at the times when you saw him?'

'Sometimes in his chart room and sometimes on the bridge, and sometimes he would come to the wheelhouse, inside of the wheelhouse.'

JGB324: 'How do you know he would go to the wheelhouse?'

'I would see him pass through.'

JGB328: 'How soon after you took your watch did you see him?'

'As near as I can tell, I saw him about 9 o'clock.'

JGB346: 'But you do know that about 9 o'clock you saw him on the deck, on the bridge, and in the wheelhouse at various times. Would you say all of the time, in one of those three places after that?'

'I did not know that the captain was anywhere away from the bridge the whole watch. I mean to say from the bridge taking the whole bridge together;

all the chart rooms, and the open bridge. They are all practically on one square, and I do not think the captain was away from that altogether.'

Captain Smith knew very well that they were entering the ice region and that this was the most dangerous part of *Titanic*'s voyage, and he remained about the bridge to supervise her navigation at this critical time.

Smith was probably resting on the settee in his chart room at the time of the collision, as he rushed fully dressed in his uniform into the wheelhouse the instant he heard the first helm order 'hard-a-starboard' and heard the iceberg scraping along *Titanic*'s hull, arriving there after the hard-a-port order had been given, whilst the noise, which only lasted a few seconds, was still continuing. We know this from the following dramatic testimony of Quartermaster Hichens, who was at *Titanic*'s helm at the time of the collision, and who testified that *Titanic* began scraping the iceberg before the helm was even hard over:

'All went along very well until 20 minutes to 12, when three gongs came from the lookout, and immediately afterwards a report on the telephone, "Iceberg right ahead." The chief officer rushed from the wing to the bridge, or I imagine so, sir. Certainly I am inclosed in the wheelhouse, and I can not see, only my compass. He rushed to the engines. I heard the telegraph bell ring; also give the order, "Hard astarboard," with the sixth officer standing by me to see the duty carried out and the quartermaster standing by my left side.

Repeated the order, "Hard astarboard. The helm is hard over, sir."'

ROH013: 'Who gave the first order?'

'Mr. Murdoch, the first officer, sir; the officer in charge. The sixth officer repeated the order, "The helm is hard astarboard, sir." But, during the time, she was crushing the ice, or we could hear the grinding noise along the ship's bottom. I heard the telegraph ring, sir. The skipper came rushing out of his [chart] room—Capt. Smith—and asked, "What is that?" Mr. Murdoch said, "An iceberg." He said, "Close the emergency doors."'

Second Officer Lightoller then observed Captain Smith keeping watch on *Titanic*'s bridge immediately after the collision, whilst the ship was slowing down:

CHL464: 'Did you see Mr. Murdoch after that?'

'Yes, sir; I saw him when I came out of the quarters after the impact.'

CHL465: 'Where was he?'

'On the bridge.'

CHL466: 'With the captain?'

'One on one side, and one on the other side of the bridge; one on each side.'

40 TITANIC COLLIDED WITH A LONE ICEBERG.

Yes, but there were dozens of icebergs, and a very large icefield in the immediate area in which *Titanic* sank. We have already heard that the lookouts could smell the ice, and—after the sinking—as soon as the cries for help of those in the water died down, Fourth Officer Joseph Groves Boxhall could hear the slight swell breaking on all the ice nearby:

> JGB845: 'Between the time that you left the *Titanic* and the time morning dawned did you see any icebergs?'
>
> 'No, sir; but I know that they were there.'
>
> JGB846: 'You knew they were there?'
>
> 'Yes; sir.'
>
> JGB847: 'Any growlers?'
>
> 'I saw nothing; but I heard the water on the ice as soon as the lights went out on the ship.'
>
> JGB848: 'That water, you think, was on the ice, after the boat went down? That is, you could hear something?'
>
> 'Yes, sir.'
>
> JGB849: 'In that vicinity?'
>
> 'A little while after the ship's lights went out and the cries subsided, then I found out that we were near the ice.'
>
> JGB850: 'You could hear it?'
>
> 'Yes.'
>
> JGB851: 'Does your statement also cover the field ice?'

'Yes; it covers all the ice, sir. I heard the water rumbling or breaking on the ice. Then I knew that there was a lot of ice about; but I could not see it from the boat.'

As the sun came up, Captain Rostron saw the extent of the ice at *Titanic*'s wreck site, from the rescue ship *Carpathia*:

25501: (The Attorney-General.) 'In the morning, when it was full daylight, did you see many icebergs?

'Yes, I sent a Junior Officer to the top of the wheelhouse, and told him to count the icebergs 150 to 200 feet high; I sampled out one or two and told him to count the icebergs of about that size. He counted 25 large ones, 150 to 200 feet high, and stopped counting the smaller ones; there were dozens and dozens all over the place; and about two or three miles from the position of the *Titanic*'s wreckage we saw a huge ice-field extending as far as we could see, N.W. to S.E.
25502: 'About two to three miles from the *Titanic*'s wreckage?

'Yes.'

Years later, Rostron told his friend Captain Barr of the Cunarder *Caronia*:

'When day broke, and I saw the ice I had steamed through during the night, I shuddered, and could only think that some other Hand than mine was on that helm during the night.'

In fact, only a few minutes' more steaming time and *Titanic* would have run into the eastern edge of this 28-mile long impenetrable barrier of field ice, which the nearby *Californian* had reached, about ten miles to the northward. We know from Walter Lord's 1957 interview with *Californian*'s Third Officer, Charles Groves, that after coming to an emergency stop, *Californian*'s Captain, Stanley Lord, then ordered a Quartermaster to bring up some coal. This he proceeded to throw over the side, onto the surrounding field ice, to see how thick it was. Satisfied that it was too thick to run through, Captain Lord decided to wait there until daylight. Had *Titanic* also made it to the edge of this enormous icefield, she would almost certainly not have sunk; and even if she had, it would have been possible to evacuate all *Titanic*'s passengers onto this thick, flat ice, possibly even using the ship's gangways to disembark her passengers. Although this sounds improbable, in 1885 the crew of a ship called the *Bayard* survived for three days on an ice floe before being rescued, after their ship struck an iceberg en route to Canada and sank.

Indeed, it is possible that a few of *Titanic*'s 1,500 victims did manage to swim to icebergs, as the following story, published in the *New York World* on April 26th, 1912, seems to confirm:

STEAMER SIGHTED HUDDLED GROUP OF DEAD ON ICEBERG

The North German Lloyd liner P*rinzess Irene*, from Genoa, reached her pier in Hoboken at 11 o'clock last night and reported that on Wednesday last she had intercepted a wireless message between two ships, the names of which were not learned, to the effect that one of them, in passing fifty miles from the scene of the *Titanic* disaster, had sighted an iceberg on which were the bodies of more than a dozen men.

All wore lifebelts and the bodies were huddled in groups at the base of the berg. It was the opinion of the officers of the ship sighting the gruesome scene that the men had climbed on the mass of ice, perhaps within an hour of the foundering of the *Titanic*, and had frozen to death as they were swept to the southward. The fact that the bodies were huddled in groups led the captain of the ship to suppose the men gathered close together to keep warm. No attempt was made to take off the bodies.

41 TITANIC STRUCK A BLUE OR DARK ICEBERG.

No. There was some discussion at the Inquiry about whether the iceberg which *Titanic* struck was a 'blue' or 'dark' iceberg. It was suggested that this appearance could have been caused by the iceberg having recently capsized. A number of witnesses had described the berg as appearing black, blue, shrouded in mist, or with only a white edge at the top. For example, Lookout Reginald Lee testified:

2441: 'It was a dark mass that came through that haze and there was no white appearing until it was just close alongside the ship, and that was just a fringe at the top.'

2442: 'It was a dark mass that appeared, you say?'

'Through this haze, and as she moved away from it, there was just a white fringe along the top. That was the only white about it, until she passed by, and then you could see she was white; one side of it seemed to be black, and the other side seemed to be white. When I had a look at it going astern it appeared to be white.'

2443: 'At that time the ship would be throwing some light upon it; there were lights on your own ship?'

'It might have been that.'

That the iceberg *Titanic* struck was in fact white is confirmed by Quartermaster Rowe, who observed the iceberg from the poop deck, as it passed along the side of the ship:

GTR026: 'Did you see any ice when on the watch?'

'No, sir; only when we struck, when we passed it on the starboard side.'

GTR027: 'About how high was that iceberg?'

'Roughly, 100 feet, sir.'

GTR028. 'Was there anything distinctive about the color of that iceberg?'

'Not a bit, sir; just like ordinary ice.'

GTR029: 'You saw it as it was brushing by?'

'Yes, sir. It was very close to the ship, almost touching it.'

The iceberg would have appeared completely white in daylight, but was hard to spot on the moonless night, with no light to reflect from its surface. We know this because *Titanic's* Fourth Officer, Joseph G. Boxhall, said that at sunrise on the morning of April 15th, 1912, he saw icebergs at *Titanic's* wreck site 'as far as the eye could see' which had been invisible in the darkness before dawn, but which had looked black when he saw them at daybreak, and white in the sunlight later on:

JGB803: 'How did this iceberg look to you? I mean as to colour?'

'White.'

JGB804: 'Did they all look about the same colour?'

'They looked white to me, in the sunlight.'

JGB805: 'Was the sun up, then?'

'No; but after the sun got up they looked white.'

JGB806: 'In the early morning, at the dawn— daybreak?'

'No; at daybreak they looked quite black.'

That white icebergs can appear completely black and invisible in the dark was confirmed by Captain Rostron of the rescue ship *Carpathia*. On the morning of April 15th, 1912, he saw a growler (small iceberg) at daylight very close to his ship which he had not seen at all in the dark:

25406: 'How close was the iceberg which you saw?'

'Well, when we had stopped, when daylight broke, it was something less than a quarter of a mile away.'

25407: 'I should like to follow that to understand it.

Had you seen that iceberg before?'

'No, it was the first I saw of it. We were close up before we saw it.'

Rostron could not account for his not having seen it before, but said that it was not a 'dark' iceberg:

25458: 'That one we understand, but this last one that you saw about 4 o'clock when you were getting ready to pick up the boat on the port side, was there anything at all special about the colour of that iceberg?'

'No, but I suppose it must have been because of the shadow or something of that kind that we could not make it out before. I cannot account for it.'

25459: 'Does it sometimes happen?'

'Yes, very often.'

25460: 'It may be, the iceberg presents to you a luminous appearance?'

'Yes.'

25461: 'Or it may be, it presents to you a dark appearance?'

'Exactly.'

25462: 'That is what you would ordinarily expect when you are looking out for icebergs, is it?'

'Yes.'

42 IF TITANIC HAD CARRIED SEARCHLIGHTS, THE LOOKOUTS WOULD HAVE SEEN THE ICE EARLIER.

Possibly. In theory, searchlights would have alerted the lookouts to the fact that *Titanic* was at that time steaming through an area containing a large number of icebergs and a large icefield, which were invisible in the calm and moonless conditions which prevailed that night, and this knowledge would have caused the Captain to order a reduction in *Titanic*'s speed.

Lightoller pointed out that although searchlights might have made a difference that night, he had little experience of them and would have to use them himself to say for sure whether they would be of use in spotting ice or whether they would make things worse. He also pointed out that they could be dangerous in narrow navigation channels to those in oncoming ships, effectively blinding them.

Capt. Francis Miller, Assistant Hydrographer to the Admiralty, thought that searchlights were of use in detecting ice and rocks, and for use in life-saving, but agreed with Lightoller that there was a considerable danger of blinding other ships, especially when not in open water. He concluded that on balance, it was better for ships not to carry them as a standard practice, although this practice was introduced after the *Titanic* disaster by the International Convention for the Safety of Life at Sea.

43 THE LOOKOUTS HAD REPORTED SEEING ICEBERGS BEFORE
THE COLLISION.

Possibly. We know from the water temperature that *Titanic*
was in the ice region from 8 p.m. and that lookout Symons
remarked to Jewell that he could actually smell the ice at 9
p.m. *Titanic* had therefore probably been passing icebergs for
more than three hours before her fatal collision at 11.40pm.
The following story, published in the *New York Herald* on
Sunday 21st April, 1912, suggests that *Titanic* steward
Thomas Whitely overheard Fleet and Lee talking about
the incident on board the *Carpathia* (though the article
erroneously concludes it was on the bottom of upturned
Collapsible B, which Whitely was rescued from!):

> 'My only information is that I heard one of the two
> men say that he had reported to the first officer that
> he saw an iceberg.'
>
> 'I heard one of them say,' he said last night in
> the hospital, 'that at a quarter after eleven o'clock on
> Sunday night, about twenty-five minutes before the
> great ship struck the berg, that he had told First Officer
> Murdoch that he believed he had seen an iceberg. He
> said he was not certain, but that he saw the outline
> of something which he thought must be a berg. A
> short time later, the lookout said, he noticed what he
> thought was another mountain of ice. Again, he called
> the attention of the first officer to it.'
>
> 'A third time he saw something in the moonlight
> (sic starlight) which he felt certain was an iceberg. The

air was cool and there were indications in his mind that there were bergs in the neighborhood. A third time he reported to the first officer that he had seen an iceberg. This time, as I recall it, he did not say merely that he fancied he saw one, but that he had actually seen one.'

'His words to the officer, as I remember them, were—"I saw the iceberg. It was very large, and to me it looked black, or rather a dark gray instead of white."'

'Mr Whiteley is not in a serious condition and will be out soon. He is a man above the average intelligence and seems very certain of what he says.'

If this report is true, it seems Murdoch believed he could see an iceberg in his path in time to avoid it, and pressed on, keeping a sharp lookout.

44 THE ICEBERG WHICH SANK THE TITANIC WAS IDENTIFIED THE DAY AFTER THE SINKING BY A SMEAR OF RED PAINT ALONG ITS SIDE.

Possibly. The *Prinz Adalbert*, a German steamer, passed near the position of *Titanic*'s sinking on April 15th and one of her passengers was photographing an iceberg when they noticed an unusual red smear around its base, which they thought meant it had been involved in a collision with a ship. On hearing later that the *Titanic* had sunk, they thought this iceberg must have been the culprit, with the red marks caused by *Titanic's* red anti-fouling paint being scraped off below her waterline during the collision.

However, another possible culprit was photographed by Stephan Rehorek, a passenger on the *Bremen* which passed close by the scene of *Titanic's* wreckage and saw hundreds of bodies in lifejackets. This picture shows signs of fresh damage at the place where the *Titanic* would have hit it according to the sketch and description of Joseph Scarrott, who described the iceberg as looking like the Rock of Gibraltar as seen from Europa Point, or something like a lion couchant, as the Wreck Commissioner Lord Mersey commented. This berg seems to fit Scarrott's description better than the *Adalbert* berg. Moreover, Colin Cooper, a passenger on the *Carpathia* and a well-known painter, also sketched an iceberg which shows damage and which fits well with Scarrott's sketch and Rehorek's picture.

Whilst it is tempting to believe these reports, several other ships in the area also reported sightings of icebergs which may have been responsible for sinking the *Titanic*. For instance, a ship called the *Cleo*, at 41' 25" N, 48' 43" W, seven miles from where the *Minia* found wreckage from the *Titanic* the following day, saw on April 29th 'a berg about 150 feet high, appearing as though it had been run into by a vessel'. Given how different icebergs look from different angles and in different lights, and given the complex currents in the area, the iceberg which actually sank the *Titanic* was never conclusively identified.

Collision

EVERYONE ON BOARD TITANIC FELT A TERRIFIC JOLT AS SHE
COLLIDED WITH THE ICEBERG.

No. As we have seen, the extreme obliqueness of the blow,
and the long distance along the hull over which the damage
occurred, combined to make the shock very light—and
often even unnoticed—in all but the most forward areas of
Titanic. For example, Leading Fireman Frederick Barrett,
who was working in No.6 Boiler Room at the time of the
collision and saw the seawater burst through the side of the
ship, compared the collision to a 'big gun' going off.

However, passengers who were further away from the
impact hardly noticed anything, and some even slept
through it. There is evidence that Colonel Archibald Gracie,
who wrote a famous account of the sinking in his 1912
book *The Truth about the Titanic*, was only awakened by the
boilers blowing off steam at about midnight, rather than by
the collision at about 11.40 p.m. Similarly, Major Arthur
Peuchen encountered two young women in First Class who
had only been awakened by Mrs Astor's voice outside their
cabins after the collision.

First Class passenger Ella White's description of the
collision is one of the more memorable:

'It did not seem to me that there was any very great impact at all. It was just as though we went over about a thousand marbles. There was nothing terrifying about it at all.'

Lady Duff Gordon was awoken by a 'grinding' sound, as she later told the *Denver Post*:

'I was asleep. The night was perfectly clear. I was awakened by a long grinding sort of shock. It was not a tremendous crash, but more as though someone had drawn a giant finger all along the side of the boat.'

The apparent gentleness of the collision may have been one reason why many passengers found it hard to believe that the ship could be seriously damaged. Lawrence Beesley, in Second Class, noticed only a slight movement of the engines and that the constant dancing of his mattress then stopped, as the engines stopped. He asked a steward what the problem was and was assured that it was nothing. The stewards probably did think at first that it was nothing serious; Steward Joseph Wheat, who had been on the *Olympic* when she threw a propeller blade, thought that was what had happened, as did George Crowe, another steward, who said that he would never have noticed the collision if he had been fully asleep.

Ship collisions with icebergs were usually not such relatively soft events. On the evening of Thursday, April 11th, 1912, the French passenger liner *Niagara* ran into an iceberg in the same icefield which would claim the *Titanic*, three days later. That accident occurred while passengers were enjoying dinner and the *New York Herald* described the dramatic encounter, as follows, on 17th April, 1912:

'Passengers were hurled headlong from their chairs and broken dishes and glass were scattered throughout the dining saloons. The next instant there was a panic among the passengers and they raced screaming and shouting to the decks. "I thought we were doomed," said Captain Juham yesterday. "At first I feared we had been in collision with another vessel as I hurried to the bridge. But when I saw it was an iceberg and that we were surrounded by ice as far as we could see through the fog, my fears for the safety of the passengers and the vessel grew. I am sure Captain Smith had a similar experience in practically the same locality when the *Titanic* went down."'

46 SOME THIRD CLASS PASSENGERS WOKE UP TO FIND THEIR CABINS AWASH.

Yes. This did happen in the case of single male steerage passengers, berthed in the forward part of *Titanic* on G deck, close to the collision point. Some of these men awoke to find the floor of their cabins awash. Third Class passenger Daniel Buckley was in one of these berths, and remembered this incident in his testimony at the US Senate inquiry:

DAB005: 'How did you happen to come over to America?'

'I wanted to come over here to make some money. I came in the *Titanic* because she was a new steamer. This night of the wreck I was sleeping in my room on the *Titanic*, in the steerage. There were three other boys from the same place sleeping in the same room with me.

'I heard some terrible noise and I jumped out on the floor, and the first thing I knew my feet were getting wet; the water was just coming in slightly. I told the other fellows to get up, that there was something wrong and, that the water was coming in. They only laughed at me. One of them says: "Get back into bed. You are not in Ireland now."

'I got on my clothes as quick as I could, and the three other fellows got out. The room was very small, so I got out, to give them room to dress themselves.

'Two sailors came along, and they were shouting: "All up on deck! unless you want to get drowned."'

47 PASSENGERS USED CHUNKS OF THE ICEBERG IN THEIR DRINKS AFTER THE COLLISION.

Possibly. It would have been possible to use pieces of the iceberg in drinks as the iceberg *Titanic* struck was made of freshwater glacier ice, and not sea ice, which is salty.

We do know that passengers handled pieces of the iceberg

following the collision. Fourth Officer Joseph Boxhall recalled, in his 1962 BBC radio interview, taking a piece of ice from a Third Class passenger; and First Class passenger Col. Archibald Gracie, in his memoir *The Truth about the Titanic*, recalled his friend James Clinch Smith (who did not survive) showing him a piece of ice shortly after the collision:

> 'I now for the first time discovered that others were aroused as well as myself, among them my friend, Clinch Smith, from whom I first learned that an iceberg had struck us. He opened his hand and showed me some ice, flat like my watch, coolly suggesting that I might take it home for a souvenir. All of us will remember the way he had of cracking a joke without a smile.'

It's possible that with freshwater glacier ice being featured in jokes such as this, and with the First Class Smoking Room still being open, passengers may well have added the odd chunk to their drinks, in the spirit of fun which still continued for many even after the collision.

However, due to the large amount of ice in the area, it was exceptionally cold on *Titanic* that night and several survivors recall drinking hot drinks at the time, such as hot toddys and even hot lemonade.

48 THE ICEBERG RIPPED A 300 FOOT GASH ALONG THE SIDE OF THE SHIP.

No. This 'fact' was a popular one in the press of the time and is one of the more enduring myths about the *Titanic*. The iceberg actually caused intermittent damage in five main places, breaching six of Titanic's watertight compartments.

Edward Wilding, one of *Titanic's* designers, estimated at the enquiry that, based on damage reports and the rate and volume of water entering the breaches, the iceberg punctured *Titanic's* hull in five main areas, and the total area of this damage was only about 12 square feet, at intervals along *Titanic's* hull from her Forepeek Tank to as far back as Boiler Room number 4:

20347: 'What I wanted to ask you is this. A difficulty is felt as to how No. 4 could have been injured in the skin of the ship if the wound terminated, as from Barrett's evidence apparently it did terminate, just above [sic *abaft*] the watertight compartment forward of No. 5?'

'From a calculation which I will refer to in a moment, I cannot believe that the wound was absolutely continuous the whole way. I believe that it was in a series of steps, and that from what we heard Barrett say in his evidence it was the end of one of the series of wounds which flooded the different spaces; that before the ship finally cleared the iceberg as the helm was put over, she would be tending to swing her side into the iceberg, and that a very light contact was made in No. 4. It seemed very probable, quite apart from actual direct evidence of the fact; that is, that after the ship had finished tearing herself at the forward end of No. 5, she would tend to push herself against the iceberg a little, or push herself up the iceberg, and there would be a certain tendency, as the stern came round to aft under the helm, to bang against the iceberg again further aft.'

20422: 'There is one other thing I think you wanted to tell us upon the points you have left. Have you made any calculation as to the volume of water that came in through the apertures of this vessel?'

'Assuming the forepeak and Nos. 1, 2 and 3 holds and No. 6 boiler room flooded…it would mean that about 16,000 tons of water had found their way into the vessel. That is the volume of the water which would have to come in. As far as I can follow from the evidence, the water was up to that level in about 40 minutes. It may be a few minutes more or less, but that was the best estimate I could make. When the inflow started the evidence we have as to the vertical position of the damage indicated that the head would be about 25 feet. Of course, as the water rose inside, that head would be reduced and the rate of inflow would be reduced somewhat. Making allowance for those, my estimate for the size of the hole required (and making some allowance for the obstruction due to the presence of decks and other things), is that the total area through which water was entering the ship, was somewhere about 12 square feet. The extent of the damage fore and aft, that is from the foremost puncture to the aftermost puncture in the cross bunker at the forward end of No. 5 boiler room, is about 500 feet [sic *200*], and the average width of the hole extending the whole way is only about three-quarters of an inch. That was my reason for stating this morning that I believe it must have been in places, that is, not a continuous rip. A hole three-quarters of an inch wide and 200 feet long does not seem to describe to me the probable damage, but it must have averaged about that amount.'

20423: 'You mean, if there was a considerably thick hole, that hole could not have gone as far along the ship as four compartments?'

'Yes, that is so. It can only have been a comparatively short length, and the aggregate of the holes must have been somewhere about 12 square feet. One cannot put it any better than that.'

20424: 'I suppose it is possible that a piece of ice made a hole and then got itself broken off?'

'Yes, quite probable.'

20425: 'And then another piece of ice made another hole, and so on?'

'Yes, that is what I believe happened.'

Titanic would have floated with her forward three watertight compartments flooded, as she was designed to do. She would even have floated that night with four flooded, Wilding estimated, based on her loading at the time and the calmness of the water. With six compartments breached, however, it was a certainty that *Titanic* would sink.

49 THE STEEL AND RIVETS USED TO MAKE TITANIC WERE OF
INFERIOR QUALITY; IF SHE'D BEEN MADE WITH BETTER METAL,
THE ICEBERG WOULDN'T HAVE SUNK HER.

No. *Titanic* was made with the same quality of steel and rivets
as the *Olympic*, which as we have seen had an extraordinarily
long and successful career. The force with which *Titanic*
struck the iceberg was easily sufficient to puncture the hull
of any ship, including a modern ship.

Although it is true that much of the damage to *Titanic*'s
hull occurred along the seams of the plates, possibly due
to the failure of the rivets holding them together, this was
simply the weakest point in a very strong structure which
was nonetheless not designed to withstand anything like the
enormous pressure exerted on the ship's hull by the iceberg.
The striking force was calculated by John Knapp, a captain in
the US Navy and a hydrographer at the Bureau of Navigation
in Washington, D.C:

'Multiplying the weight of the ship by the square of
its speed in feet per second and dividing by twice the
force of gravity will give the blow that would have been
struck if she had kept straight on her course against
this apparently solid mass of ice, which, at a speed of
21 knots, would have been equal to 1,173,200 foot
tons, or energy enough to lift 14 monuments the size
of the Washington Monument in one second of time.
I think from the evidence before your committee it
is shown that the ship struck the berg before she had
appreciably lost any headway, due either to change

of helm or stoppage or reversal of engines, in which event her striking energy would be practically that given above.'

Even assuming *Titanic* was constructed of the very highest quality steel available today, this enormous force would still have bent her plates and popped her rivets.

50 IF THE BULKHEADS OF TITANIC'S WATERTIGHT COMPARTMENTS HAD BEEN HIGHER SHE WOULDN'T HAVE SUNK.

No. Six of her forward watertight compartments were flooded, all the way back to her No. 4 boiler room; with this amount of underwater damage, *Titanic* would have sunk even if her bulkheads had gone all the way up to the top of the ship, as Edward Wilding, one of *Titanic*'s designers, confirmed at the British Inquiry:

> 20953: 'If No. 6 boiler room and the compartments forward of it are flooded, am I right that the vessel, as she is designed, is lost—she must sink?'
> 'If No. 6 boiler room and the three holds forward of it, and the forepeak are flooded, the ship is undoubtedly lost as built.'
> 20954: 'If No. 5 boiler room is flooded in addition, supposing the bulkheads had been carried up to D, would that have saved her?'

'It would not.'

'And the last question is: With No. 4 section added on, no possible arrangement could save the ship?'

'No possible vertical extension of the existing bulkheads.'

51 IF TITANIC HAD HAD LONGITUDINAL BULKHEADS, THESE WOULD HAVE CONTAINED THE WATER AND STOPPED THE SHIP FROM SINKING.

Probably not. Cunard's *Mauretania* and *Lusitania* were built with government subsidy on the understanding that they could be used as troop transport ships in wartime and were therefore fitted with the longitudinal watertight bulkheads which military ships were required to have, as well as transverse bulkheads like *Titanic*'s.

Longitudinal bulkheads would theoretically have saved *Titanic*, but having them would also have meant she would have developed a severe list to starboard. Wilding calculated that *Titanic*'s damage would have caused the *Mauretania* to list by 22 degrees. This would not necessarily have sunk the *Mauretania*, but it is interesting to note that this list would have rendered 50% of the lifeboats carried by either ship unusable—which is precisely what happened when the *Lusitania* was sunk by a torpedo in 1915. A list might also, in some situations, make flooding worse. As Wilding pointed out at the British Enquiry, if the vessel lists, this brings the top of the transverse bulkheads closer to the waterline and therefore increases the danger of letting water in:

> 20420: 'As I understand, the danger indicated there is that if the vessel lists, among other things, that will reduce at the side the height of the transverse watertight compartment?'
> 'Reduce at the side the height of the top of the transverse bulkheads above water.'
> 20421: 'It might bring it below the waterline?'
> 'Yes, and thus let the water get along the deck.'

It was therefore considered that in most situations longitudinal bulkheads would be more harmful than helpful. Indeed, as First Class passenger Grace Scott Bowen testified at the Limited Liability Hearings into the disaster in 1915, many portholes were left open as *Titanic* sank and this would have increased the speed at which she sank had she been fitted with longitudinal bulkheads, as these would have increased her initial list and brought more portholes under water more quickly:

> Q: 'Did you notice anything about the portholes as your boat went down, or after it got in the water?'
> 'After we got in the water I noticed many were open.'
> Q: 'Did you notice any circular portholes open?'
> 'Yes.'
> Q: 'Square ones, also?'
> 'I think so.'
> Q: 'How many lines of portholes did you notice when

your boat got into the water?'

'Two.'

Q: 'Were any of those submerged after you got in the boat?'

'Gradually this one line disappeared.'

Q: 'You saw the water going in?'

'Yes.'

Q: 'Were a few of them open, or many open?'

'I should say a great many.'

52 IF TITANIC HAD RAMMED THE ICEBERG HEAD-ON, SHE WOULD HAVE SURVIVED.

Yes, she probably would have done, as one of *Titanic*'s designer's, Edward Wilding, explained in the following fascinating exchange at the British Inquiry:

20266: 'Perhaps I ought to put this general question to you. The contact with this iceberg was the contact of a body weighing 50,000 tons moving at the rate of 22 knots an hour?'

'Yes.'

20267: 'I gather to resist such a contact as that you could not build any plates strong enough, as plates?

'It depends, of course, on the severity of the contact. This contact seems to have been a particularly light one.'

20268: 'Light?'

'Yes, light, because we have heard the evidence that lots of people scarcely felt it.'

20269: 'You mean it did not strike a fair blow?'

'If she struck it a fair blow I think we should have heard a great deal more about the severity of it, and probably the ship would have come into harbour if she had struck it a fair blow, instead of going to the bottom.'

20270: 'You think that?'

'I am quite sure of it.'

20271: (The Commissioner.) 'I am rather interested about that. Do you mean to say that if this ship had driven on to the iceberg stem on she would have been saved?'

'I am quite sure she would, My Lord. I am afraid she would have killed every fireman down in the firemen's quarters, but I feel sure the ship would have come in.'

20272: 'And the passengers would not have been lost?'

'The passengers would have come in.'

20273: 'Then do you think it was an error of judgment—to starboard the helm?'

'I do not by any means say it was a negligent act at all. It is very difficult to pass judgment on what would go through an Officer's mind, My Lord.'

20274: 'An error of judgment and negligence are two different things altogether. A man may make a mistake and be very far from being negligent?'

'Yes.'

20275: 'Do you think that if the helm had not been starboarded there would have been a chance of the ship being saved?'

'I believe the ship would have been saved, and I am strengthened in that belief by the case which your Lordship will remember where one large North Atlantic steamer, some 34 years ago, did go stem on into an iceberg and did come into port, and she was going fast?'

'I am old enough to remember that case, but I am afraid my memory is not good enough.'

Mr. Laing: 'The *Arizona*—I remember it.'

The Witness: 'The *Arizona*, my Lord.'

20276: (Mr. Rowlatt) 'You said it would have killed all the firemen?'

'I am afraid she would have crumpled up in stopping herself. The momentum of the ship would have crushed in the bows for 80 or perhaps 100 feet.'

20277: 'You mean the firemen in their quarters?'

'Yes, down below. We know two watches were down there.'

20278: 'Do you mean at the boilers?'

'Oh, no, they would scarcely have felt the shock.'

The Commissioner: 'Any person, fireman or anybody else, who happened to be in that 100 feet, would probably never have been seen again?'

20279: (Mr. Rowlatt) 'The third class passengers are there too, I think, some of them?'

'I do not think there are any third class passengers forward of the second bulkhead, and I believe she would have stopped before the second bulkhead was damaged. It is entirely crew there, and almost entirely firemen—firemen, trimmers, and greasers.'

20280: 'Your opinion is that the ship would have suffered that crushing in in the first two compartments, but that the shock would not have shattered or loosened the rivets in any other part of the ship?'

'Not sufficiently. As it would take a considerable length, 80 or 100 feet to bring up, it is not a shock, it is a pressure that lasts three or four seconds, five seconds perhaps, and whilst it is a big pressure it is not in the nature of a sharp blow.'

20281: (The Commissioner) 'It would, I suppose, have shot everybody in the ship out of their berths?'

'I very much doubt it, My Lord.'

20282: 'At 22 1/2 knots an hour, and being pulled up quite suddenly?'

'Not quite suddenly, My Lord. 100 feet will pull up a motor car going 22 miles an hour without shooting you out of the front.'

20283: (Mr. Rowlatt) 'What you mean is that the ship would have telescoped herself?'

'Yes, up against the iceberg.'

20284: 'And stopped when she telescoped enough?'

'Yes, that is what happened in the *Arizona*.'

53 ENGINEERS AND STOKERS WERE TRAPPED BELOW BY
THE WATERTIGHT DOORS AS THEY CAME DOWN AFTER THE
COLLISION.

No. *Titanic's* doors closed relatively slowly and every
watertight compartment had its own escape ladder, for use
both to evacuate and gain access to these compartments after
the watertight doors had closed.

However, one man was trapped briefly. He was a tunnel
greaser who looked after the propeller shafts at the stern of the
ship and although there was an escape ladder, he apparently
was not aware of it and had to be rescued by greaser Frederick
Scott and others. Each watertight door could be opened by
hand even after they had been closed automatically from the
bridge, and this is how the greaser was rescued. Subsequently
Scott and his colleagues were told by the engineer on watch
in the turbine room to pull up all the watertight doors so
the suction hoses could be brought through, in an attempt
to stem the flood of water coming in, as greaser Frederick
Scott's testimony shows:

5546: (The Attorney-General, Sir Rufus Isaacs) 'Then
the next thing that happened was something with
reference to the watertight doors?'

Mr Scott: 'Yes, the watertight doors all closed.'

5547: (Sir Rufus) 'Did you hear any bell ring first?'

Mr Scott: 'No, not for the watertight doors.'

5548: (Sir Rufus) 'Do you mean that without any
signal they came down?'

Mr Scott: 'Yes.'

5549: (Sir Rufus) 'Which watertight doors are you speaking of?'

Mr Scott: 'All of them.'

5550: (Sir Rufus) 'When you say "all of them," how many do you mean?'

Mr Scott: 'I think it is about six, leading down to the afterend of the tunnel.'

5551: (Sir Rufus) 'Do you mean not only in your engine room, but you are speaking also of what you could see aft; the other watertight doors had been open?'

Mr Scott: 'We had to go and open them up afterwards.'

5552: (Sir Rufus) 'I understand now what you mean. You are standing in the turbine engine room and there you have got watertight doors fore and aft which were open, and aft you could see the other watertight doors were open?'

Mr Scott: 'Yes.'

5553: (Sir Rufus) 'Then, if I follow you correctly, what happened was, all those doors closed down at the same time?'

Mr Scott: 'Yes.'

5554: (Sir Rufus) 'What did you do after that?'

Mr Scott: 'After that we went up to the turbine room and down one of the escapes to let one of the greasers out in the after tunnel.

5555: (Sir Rufus) 'That is into the electric room?'

Mr Scott: 'No, there is another tunnel after that one.'

5556: (Sir Rufus) 'Do you mean the aftermost one?'

Mr Scott: 'Yes, the aftermost one of the lot.'

5557: (Sir Rufus) 'That is the very last on the tank top, your Lordship will see. (To the Witness) You went there?'

Mr Scott: 'Yes, and heaved the door up about two feet to let the greaser out.'

5558: (Sir Rufus) 'Who was the greaser there?'

Mr Scott: 'He was tunnel greaser, the one who looks after the tunnel.'

5559: (Sir Rufus) 'You had to release him?'

Mr Scott: 'We had to go and heave the door up.'

5560: (Sir Rufus) 'Did you hear any message given by the Chief Engineer [Joseph Bell] to release the watertight doors?'

Mr Scott: 'No.'

5570: (Sir Rufus) 'To release the clutch?'

Mr Scott: 'No. After we got the greaser out we came back to the turbine-room again, and the Engineer in the turbine-room told us to heave up all the watertight doors. That was after we came back from letting the greaser out of the tunnel. '

54 TITANIC SANK MORE RAPIDLY BECAUSE HER WATERTIGHT DOORS WERE OPENED AGAIN AFTER THE COLLISION.

No. It is true that most of *Titanic's* watertight doors were opened about an hour after the collision by the engineers, in order to bring pipes from the powerful pumps in the stern to bear at the bow where seawater was flooding in fast. These were never closed again:

5599: 'And you left all those doors open?'

'All those doors open.'

The Commissioner: 'Then all the watertight doors aft of the main engine room were opened?'

5600: (The Attorney-General) 'Yes. (To the Witness) And, so far as you know, as I understand it, they never were closed?'

'No. Why they opened them was they had to go down the last tunnel but one and get a big suction-pipe out, which they used for drawing the water up out of the bilges.'

5601: 'That tunnel is the one before you get to the last watertight door where they went to get a big suction pipe?'

'Yes, it takes four men to carry it. I think I saw four men coming through with it. They took it to the stokehold. What they did with it I do not know.'

The Commissioner: 'Will you get what time this was?'

5602: (The Attorney-General, to the Witness) 'What time was it?'

'About a quarter to one.'

5603: (The Commissioner) 'That is about an hour after the collision?'

'Yes.'

5604: (The Attorney-General) 'When you came back to the main engine room did you see whether the watertight doors forward of the main engine room were open?'

'They must have been, because they could not take a suction pipe out to the stokehold if they were not.'

However, this did not have a significant impact upon the amount of time *Titanic* stayed afloat, as all her watertight doors had floats which made the doors shut automatically on contact with water:

Mr. Laing [counsel questioning greaser Frederick Scott]: 'May I interpose here and say that these watertight doors are fitted with a float so that if any material quantity of water comes the float automatically releases the door and it comes down again by itself.'

Titanic's watertight doors were capable of closing against a full inrush of water, as they did in the case of *Olympic*'s collision with HMS *Hawke*, as Wilding testified:

20445: 'I think your model is sufficient. In the first place, you have spoken of the descending door. Supposing that water was gaining access into the compartment on one side of the door in volume, so that there was water flowing along rapidly, would that stop the door descending?'

'It would not; we have had proof that it would not.'

20446: 'You have had proof?'

'Quite.'

20447: 'In what way?'

'In the case of the *Olympic* accident. A stoker was standing by the door in O bulkhead in the tunnel in the aftermost section of the tunnel, forward of the propeller here. (Pointing on the model.) It was put in evidence at the *Olympic* trial, and can be turned up therefore, that he saw the ram come through, and as the ship drifted out he saw the water come in with a rush; the automatic release from the bridge had not yet been worked, and he took the hand lever, standing on the fore side of the door, and released that door, and it fell and closed properly, but during the time it took to do so sufficient water had come through the door to bring about 3 feet of water into the next forward section of the tunnel—some 300 or 400 tons of water had come through. The door closed, and the water was pumped out; so that it closed against the rush of water.

Indeed, *Titanic*'s watertight doors were so heavy that they could even cut through coal, if necessary, in order to close, and a suction pipe would not have prevented them sealing:

20438: 'Supposing at the bottom there was a little bit

of coal or something which prevented it getting quite down?'

'The door is falling; it is falling freely until it overlaps that place, and the door would smash through any small thing. This is not a very big model, but it will smash through a lead pencil if I let it go.'

20439: 'Supposing the door, having overlapped the step at the bottom still nevertheless is prevented by some little obstacle from getting down quite as far as is intended?'

'As this is falling with a rush, until the wedges actually press it home, the distance through which there is contact is only a matter of an inch or so - except just during that last inch when the door is stopped—the weight of the door would be sufficient to clear any obstacle.

20440: 'Overcome anything like a piece of coal?'

'Yes; it would simply knock it out of the way. Some of the big doors weigh, I think, 15 cwt., three-quarters of a ton, so that it would want a pretty substantial obstacle.'

SOS

55 TITANIC DID NOT SEND A DISTRESS SIGNAL UNTIL 47 MINUTES AFTER THE COLLISION.

Yes. In 1912 ships' clocks were set at midnight to correspond to the longitude of where the ship was expected to be at noon the following day, when the sun would be directly overhead, with adjustments made in the morning according to the speed of the ship. *Titanic's* noon position on 14th April, 1912 was 43.02N 44.31W.

We know this because we know that *Titanic* was following the normal steamship route westwards along the south coast of Ireland from Daunt's Rock Lightship at 51.43N 8.16W to Fastnet Light at 51.23N 9.36W, and from there she was following the Great Circle (or shortest) route westwards to a point in the Atlantic known as The Corner, at 42N 47W, where westbound steamships at that time of the year then turned due west to follow a Rhumb Line course to the approaches to New York harbour. The distance along this standardised westbound steamer route from Daunt's Rock Lightship to The Corner was 1,675 miles and we know from Titanic's daily ship's run data provided by Third Officer Pitman that *Titanic* had run (484 + 519 + 546 =) 1,549 nautical miles along this route at noon on Sunday 14th April,

1912. (This means that at noon she had 1,675 − 1,549 = 126 miles to go to The Corner and this figure agrees with *Titanic* reaching The Corner at 5.50 p.m. or 350 minutes later, as we know she did, as 126/350 x 60 = 21.6 knots, which was about *Titanic's* average speed that afternoon).

By plotting this point along that track we can see that *Titanic* was at longitude 44.31W at noon on Sunday 14th April 1912. This longitude is 30 degrees and 29 minutes of arc east of New York at 75W, because there are 60 minutes of arc in one degree of arc (so 75 degrees − 44 degrees and 31 minutes = 30 degrees and 29 minutes).

Given that the sun takes 24 hours to circle 360 degrees of arc around the globe, it travels (360/24=) 15 degrees of arc every hour, or (15x60=) 900 minutes of arc every hour, or (900/60=) 15 minutes of arc every one minute of time, or one minute of arc every (60/15=) four seconds. Therefore, the sun would take two hours, one minute and 56 seconds to travel the 30 degrees and 29 minutes of arc from *Titanic's* noon position on 14th April to New York, whose time is measured from 75W ((**2 hours** x 15 degrees of arc = 30 degrees) + (**1 minute** of time x 15 minutes of arc = 15 minutes of arc) + (**56 seconds**/4 = 14 minutes of arc) = 30 degrees and 29 minutes).

Thus *Titanic's* clocks were about two hours and two minutes ahead of New York time. This was confirmed by Harold Bride during the following testimony at the US Inquiry, though he did not go into the detail of the one minute and 56 seconds, content with correcting Senator Fletcher that the difference was not 1 hour and 55 minutes, but about 2 hours:

HSB709: 'Did you have a watch or clock in your room?'

'We had two clocks, sir.'

HSB710: 'Were they both running?'

'Yes, sir; one was keeping New York time and the other was keeping ship's time.'

HSB711: (Senator Fletcher) 'The difference was about 1 hour and 55 minutes?'

'There was about two hours' difference between the two.'

Now *Titanic* did not adjust her clocks again at midnight on Sunday night, as she would normally have done. This was because, in the words of Third Officer Pitman:

HJP643: 'When were the ship's clocks set; do you know?'

'They are set at midnight every night.'

HJP645: 'And were they set at midnight Sunday night?'

'No; we had something else to think of.'

We also know that *Titanic*'s first distress signal was picked up by Cape Race and others at 10.25pm New York time. This was therefore 12.27 a.m. on *Titanic*, 47 minutes after her collision at 11.40 p.m.

56 TITANIC WAS THE FIRST SHIP TO USE THE DISTRESS SIGNAL
SOS.

No. SOS was probably first used on 10th June 1909, about
three years before the *Titanic* sank, by the Cunard liner SS
Slavonia, when she was wrecked off the Azores.

It is sometimes claimed that the first SOS call was in fact
sent in January of that year by the White Star liner RMS
Republic, on January 23rd, 1909, after she accidentally
rammed the SS *Florida*. However, the call used in this case
was not SOS but the original Marconi distress signal CQD,
making the *Republic's* claim to fame being possibly the first
use of any distress call by wireless transmission. CQD,
transmitted in Morse code as:

—.—. ——.— —..

was one of the first distress signals adopted for radio use. It
was announced on January 7, 1904, by Circular 57 of the
Marconi International Marine Communication Company,
and became effective, for Marconi installations, beginning
February 1, 1904.

Contrary to popular belief, CQD does not stand for
'Come Quick, Danger' or 'Come Quickly Distress'. Land
telegraphs had traditionally used 'CQ' to identify messages
of interest to all stations along a telegraph line, and CQ
had also been adopted as a 'general call' for maritime radio
use. The CQ call was originally used by landline telegraphy
operators in the United Kingdom. French was, and still is,
the official language for international postal services, and the

word sécurité was used to mean 'safety' or 'pay attention'. It is still used in this sense in international telecommunications. The letters CQ, when pronounced in French, resemble the first two syllables of sécurité, and were therefore used as shorthand for the word. In English-speaking countries, the origin of the abbreviation CQ was popularly changed to the phrase 'seek you'. However, in landline usage there was no general emergency signal, so the Marconi company added a 'D' to CQ in order to create its distress call. Thus 'CQD' meant literally, 'All stations: distress.'

There is evidence that the German Imperial Navy Office, or 'Reichs-Marineamt' had designated the signal

$$\cdots - - - \cdots \text{ (SOS)}$$

to be the official distress signal for all German ship and coastal radio stations as early as April 1904. Certainly, SOS was referred to as a distress signal in Germany as part of a set of national radio regulations which came into effect from April 1, 1905. These regulations formally introduced three Morse code sequences, including the SOS distress signal:

1.   Ruhezeichen ('Cease-sending signal'), consisting of six dahs ($- - - - - -$), sent by shore stations to tell other local stations to stop transmitting.

2.   Suchzeichen ('Quest signal'), composed of three-dits/three dahs/one-dit, all run together ($\cdots - - - \cdot$), used by ships to get the attention of shore stations.

3.   Notzeichen ('Distress signal'), consisting of three-dits/three-dahs/three-dits ($\cdots$ — — — $\cdots$), also in a continuous sequence, to be repeated by a ship in distress until all other stations have stopped.

So the SOS distress signal was simply the adding of two dits to the general German radio call or 'Quest signal':

$$\cdots - - - \cdot$$

to make

$$\cdots - - - \cdots$$

a simple and distinctive distress communication.

It was decided that SOS should become the worldwide standard distress signal at the Second International Radiotelegraphic Convention in Berlin on November 3rd, 1906. This came into effect on July 1, 1908, with Article XVI of the regulations adopting Germany's 'Notzeichen', or distress signal, as the international standard, saying: 'Ships in distress shall use the following signal: $\cdots$ — — — $\cdots$ repeated at brief intervals.'

In both the April 1st, 1905 German law, and the 1906 International regulations, the distress signal was specified as a continuous Morse code sequence of three-dits/three-dahs/three-dits, with no mention of any alphabetic equivalents. However, in International Morse, three dits comprise the letter S, and three dahs the letter O, so it was therefore easiest to refer to the distress signal as 'SOS', and an early report on The International Radio-Telegraphic Convention in the January 12th, 1907 edition of Electrical World stated that, 'Vessels in distress use the special signal, SOS, repeated at short intervals.' In popular usage, SOS became associated with phrases such as 'save our ship' or 'save our souls', but these were only conceived of by English speaking countries after the signal had been adopted, as an aid to remembering the correct letters.

In 1912, *Titanic* sent both the traditional Marconi distress signal CQD and the new international distress signal SOS, because when Captain Smith came into *Titanic*'s Marconi room a second time and asked 'What are you sending?' Phillips replied, 'CQD' and Bride quipped:

> 'Send SOS; it's the new call, and it may be your last chance to send it!'

This well-timed joke made him and Phillips and Captain Smith all laugh, momentarily relieving the terrible stress of their situation.

57 TITANIC'S DISTRESS SIGNAL GAVE THE WRONG POSITION.

Yes. At about 7.30 p.m., Lightoller took a set of star sights in order to calculate *Titanic*'s position. Third officer Pitman recorded the timings of these stellar observations on a small deck watch, but it is likely that at this point he made an error, only recently discovered by *Titanic* expert Sam Halpern, of one minute of time when translating these star sight timings to *Titanic*'s ship's chronometer time.

Boxhall then worked out *Titanic*'s position using this incorrect timing data, which therefore resulted in an error of 15 minutes of arc of longitude, giving a position approximately 13 miles too far west. Because the error was only one of timing and not of celestial observation it affected all of the star observations equally, and thus they all agreed, apparently confirming the incorrect result, which therefore went unnoticed.

James Moore, captain of the *Mount Temple*, which also rushed to *Titanic*'s aid that night, testified that he had received two different distress positions from *Titanic*:

'The first position I got was 41° 46' N., 50° 24' W. It was afterwards corrected to 41° 44' N. and 50° 14' W.'

However, neither of these positions was anywhere near correct, as Dr Robert Ballard proved when he discovered the wreck in 1985 at 41' 43' N, 49' 56' W, thirteen miles east of the final distress position given by *Titanic*. This mistake was one reason that the wreck was not found until 73 years after the sinking.

Boxhall was so sure of his position that he asked that his ashes be scattered at the second CQD position after his death in 1967; he never knew that the ship in fact sank 13 miles east of it, though he should have noticed at the time that his carefully calculated position was unusually far ahead of *Titanic*'s Dead Reckoning position for 8 p.m. ship's time.

Captain Moore testified at the time that he thought *Titanic's* CQD position was at least eight miles too far west, since, when he arrived at her reported position, he found himself on the west side of the ice barrier running north/south; *Titanic*, coming from the east, could only have been on the east side of this barrier. Moore was therefore aware of *Titanic's* navigational mistake at the time, but his evidence was discounted in the light of Boxhall's evidence that his star sight calculations all agreed with each other, together with the fact that *Carpathia* came across *Titanic's* lifeboats using Boxhall's position. In fact, it was pure luck that *Carpathia's* path to the incorrect distress position just happened to bring her across *Titanic's* actual wreck site.

58 CARPATHIA WAS THE FIRST SHIP TO PICK UP TITANIC'S DISTRESS SIGNAL.

No. The passenger steamer *Mount Temple* and the Marconi shore station at Cape Race were the first to receive *Titanic's* distress signal, 41° 46' N, 50° 24' W, at about 10.25 p.m. New York time. But about 10 minutes later *Titanic* sent out a revised distress position, 41° 44' N, 50° 14' W.

We now know that both these positions were incorrect by several miles, but we also know that it was only this second position which Harold Cottam first picked up on the *Carpathia*, after he happened to call *Titanic* just before he went to bed to let her know that there were messages waiting for her at Cape Race. Cottam had in fact been out of his wireless room, reporting the day's communications to the officers on *Carpathia*'s bridge, when *Titanic* sent out her first distress signals:

> 17102: 'I wrote out the chit of the previous communications during the day and reported them to the bridge. After reporting them I returned to the cabin, and I sat down, and I asked the *Titanic* if he was aware there was a batch of messages coming through from Cape Cod for him, and his only answer was, "Struck a berg; come at once."'
>
> 17103: 'Now tell us, as nearly as you can, it is only a recollection, I understand—what it was which the *Titanic* said to you?'
>
> 'She said, "Come at once; we have struck a berg," and sent his position, and then he sent C.Q.D.'

Harold Cottam on the *Carpathia* was thus alerted to the tragedy unfolding on *Titanic*. It is interesting to note that, had Cottam not taken it upon himself to call the *Titanic* about this general piece of business before he went to bed (which he only did casually as he was untying his boots, before turning off his wireless for the night), it would have been the *Californian* which rescued all *Titanic*'s survivors from her lifeboats, at 8.30am, and not the *Carpathia*, four hours earlier.

59 THE FRANKFURT, 150 MILES AWAY, WAS TOLD, 'YOU FOOL, STANDBY AND KEEP OUT,' WHEN SHE CONTACTED TITANIC.

Yes. However, this was in response to the *Frankfurt's* question 'What's up old man?', which Phillips received at 2 a.m., immediately after Captain Smith had told him and Bride to abandon their cabin. Some of the events leading up to Phillip's rude reply are explained here, in the following extract from a report by Harold Bride to the Marconi traffic manager, Mr W.R. Cross, written on 27th April, 1912:

'The noise of escaping steam directly over our cabin caused a deal of trouble to Mr. Phillips in reading the replies to our distress call, and this I also reported to Capt. Smith, who by some means managed to get it abated.

'The *Olympic* next answered our call, but as far as I know, Mr. Phillips did not go to much trouble with her, as we now realized the awful state of affairs, the ship listing heavily to port and forward.

'The captain also came in and told us she was sinking fast and could not last longer than half an hour.

'Mr. Phillips then went outside to see how things were progressing, and meanwhile I established communication with the *Baltic*, telling him we were in urgent need of assistance.

'This I reported to Mr. Phillips on his return, but suggested "MBC" was too far away to be of any use.

'Mr. Phillips told me the forward well deck was

under water, and we got our lifebelts out and tied on each other, after putting on additional clothing.

'Again Mr. Phillips called "CQD" and "SOS" and for nearly five minutes got no reply, and then both the *Carpathia* and the *Frankfurt* called.

'Just at this moment the captain came into the cabin and said, "You can do nothing more; look out for yourselves." Mr. Phillips resumed the phones and after listening a few seconds jumped up and fairly screamed, "The ----- fool. He says, 'What's up old man?'" I asked "Who?" Mr. Phillips replied the *Frankfurt* and at that time it seemed perfectly clear to us that the *Frankfurt*'s operator had taken no notice or misunderstood our first call for help.

'Mr. Philips reply to this was "You fool, stbdi [sic stbdi, standby] and keep out."'

Titanic expert George Behe points out that in fact the *Frankfurt*'s operator, W Zippel, was well aware of *Titanic*'s plight at this stage, but it appears that *Titanic*'s wireless transmitter had badly lost power at 1.35 a.m. and *Frankfurt* and other ships had lost contact with *Titanic* at this time; although *Titanic*'s ability to transmit messages was curtailed, her ability to receive messages continued unabated. Zippel's words, which so much angered Phillips, were therefore just his attempt to contact *Titanic* after she had appeared to remain radio silent for so long. Zippel apparently did not receive *Titanic*'s angry reply, due again to *Titanic*'s problems with transmitting at this stage in her sinking.

Behe's research, published in *The Titanic Commutator*,

the official magazine of the Titanic Historical Society, also revealed that, like the *Carpathia's*, the *Frankfurt's* initial contact with *Titanic* at 12.20 a.m. was a routine one, and was not in response to *Titanic's* distress signals (which the *Frankfurt* had not picked up by that time). However, Phillips understandably assumed that the *Frankfurt's* routine communication was a response to his distress signal, so simply replied, "Go and get your position". This Zippel, equally understandably, assumed was therefore a request for a routine exchange of ships' positions, known as a 'time rush,' in the Marconi terminology of the day.

Zippel therefore casually replied, 'OK. Stand by,' and went off to get the *Frankfurt's* latest position from the bridge, noting in his wireless log:

'Communication with steamship *Titanic* bound west, nil.'

A full 16 minutes later, at 12.36 a.m., Zippel sent Phillips the *Frankfurt's* position and Phillips replied: 'Are you coming to our assistance?' A startled Zippel then asked, 'What is the matter with you?' However, Phillips did not get angry at this question, probably because he realised that a misunderstanding had occurred, and replied: 'We have collision with iceberg; Sinking; Please tell your captain to come.' Now realising the true situation, Zippel immediately replied: 'OK. Will tell bridge right away.' And ran to the bridge, where he persuaded Captain Hattorff to go immediately to *Titanic's* aid.

However, neither of these unfortunate misunderstandings affected the outcome of the *Titanic* disaster, as the *Frankfurt* was about 150 miles away from the *Titanic*, about three times further than *Titanic*'s eventual rescue ship *Carpathia*.

60 TITANIC'S DISTRESS MESSAGE WAS PICKED UP ON THE ROOF OF A NEW YORK DEPARTMENT STORE.

No. David Sarnoff, a radio operator who worked for Wanamaker's in New York, did relay messages from the *Olympic* and the *Carpathia*, but this was later on in the day, after *Titanic* had sunk and when the news had already spread.

Philip Franklin, vice-president of the International Mercantile Marine which owned the White Star Line, was woken by a reporter at 2.30 a.m. New York Time on April 15th, saying that they had received information from the *Virginian* via Montreal that *Titanic* had struck an iceberg and was sinking. This was then confirmed by the Associated Press. When Franklin reached the White Star Line office, he found this memorandum:

'*Titanic*. Received from Associated Press from Cape Race 3.05 a.m. Monday, April 15. 10.25 p.m. E. S. T., *Titanic* called CQD; reported having struck iceberg and required immediate assistance. Half an hour afterwards, reported that they were sinking by the head. Women were being put off in boats and weather calm and clear. Gave position as 41.46 north, 50.14 west. Stop. This station notified Allan liner *Virginian*, who immediately advised he was proceeding toward scene of disaster. Stop. *Virginian* at midnight stated was about 170 miles distant from *Titanic* and expected reach there about 10 a.m. *Olympic*, at 4.24 p.m. G. M. T. in latitude 40.32 north, longitude 61.18 west, was in direct communication with *Titanic* and is now making all haste toward her. *Baltic*, at 1.15 a.m. E. S. T. reported himself as about 200 miles east of *Titanic*, and was also making toward her. Last signals from *Titanic* were heard by *Virginian* at 12.25 a.m. E. S. T. He reported them blurred and ending abruptly.'

The Olympic sent the following message before 2.40am saying:

HADDOCK, *Olympic*:
'Thanks, your message. We have received nothing from *Titanic* but rumored that she proceeding slowly *Halifax*, but we can not confirm this. We expect *Virginian* alongside *Titanic*. Try and communicate her.'

No-one at White Star Line in New York realised the extent of the disaster for most of the day, and nor did many of the newspapers, which mostly carried very cautious headlines saying that there had been an accident and reporting what the White Star Line had heard from the Associated Press via the *Virginian* and Cape Race. She was thought unsinkable, admitted Franklin, and the White Star Line had therefore not dreamed there was a serious loss of life. A special train had even been laid on by the White Star Line to take relatives to Halifax to meet the ship. The daughter of First Class passengers Isidor and Ida Straus was on this train, knowing nothing of what had really happened, when it was suddenly reversed and she was told that *Titanic*'s passengers were instead coming to New York. That evening, a delayed message from the *Olympic* was received which broke the news, as Franklin related:

> PAF111: 'Now, at about 6.20 or 6.30pm, April 15th, the following telegram was handed to me.'
> PAF112: 'By whom, and where were you?'
> 'Handed to me by Mr. Toppin at No. 9 Broadway.'
> PAF113: 'Who is he?'
> 'Assistant to the vice president.'

The record here shows this was received at 6.16 P.M. This is addressed to Ismay, New York, and is as follows:

> '*Carpathia* reached *Titanic*'s position at daybreak. Found boats and wreckage only. *Titanic* had foundered about 2.20am in 41.16 north, 50.14 west. All her boats accounted for. About 675 souls saved, crew and passengers, latter nearly all women and children. Leyland Line S. S. *Californian* remaining and searching position of disaster. *Carpathia* returning to New York with survivors; please inform Cunard. HADDOCK.'

Ismay had in fact sent the following message from the

Carpathia on the morning of the 15th, but it didn't reach New York until the 17th:

> 'Deeply regret advise you *Titanic* sank this morning after collision iceberg, resulting serious loss life. Full particulars later.'

After he received *Olympic's* message, Franklin then invited the waiting press into his office, as he testified at the US enquiry:

> PAF114: 'That is from the captain of the *Olympic*?'
> 'Of the *Olympic*.'
> PAF115: 'Addressed to Ismay?'
> 'New York; that is our cable address. Immediately that telegram was received by me it was such a terrible shock that it took us a few minutes to get ourselves together. Then at once I telephoned, myself, to two of our directors, Mr. Steele and Mr. Morgan, jr., and at the same time sent downstairs for the reporters. I started to read the message, holding it in my hands, to the reporters. I got off the first line and a half, where it said, "The *Titanic* sank at 2 o'clock a.m.," and there was not a reporter left in the room—they were so anxious to get out to telephone the news.'

The *Californian* Incident

61 THE CALIFORNIAN WAS ABOUT 20 MILES AWAY FROM THE SINKING TITANIC.

No, the stationary *Californian* was only about 10 miles away to the northwards of the sinking *Titanic* all night. We know this because she was still there at daybreak, observed from *Titanic*'s wreck site by Second Officer James Bisset of the rescue ship *Carpathia*, as he described in his book *Tramps and Ladies*, based on the diary he kept in 1912:

> 'While we had been picking up the survivors, in the slowly increasing daylight after 4:30 a.m., we had sighted the smoke of a steamer on the fringe of the pack ice, ten miles away from us to the northwards. She was making no signals, and we paid little attention to her, for we were occupied with more urgent matters, but at 6 a.m., we had noticed that she was under way and slowly coming towards us.
>
> 'When I took over the watch on the bridge of the *Carpathia* at 8 a.m., the stranger was little more than a mile from us, and flying her signals of identification. She was the Leyland Line cargo steamer *Californian*, which had been stopped overnight...'

However, the British Inquiry concluded that *Californian* was even nearer, estimating the distance at only about 5-7 miles rather than the 15-19 miles of Captain Lord's testimony. This was because several witnesses on the *Titanic*, including her Navigating Officer, Fourth Officer Boxhall, concluded that the *Californian* must have been only about 5 miles away due to the clarity of her lights that night.

That *Californian* had in fact been lying only about 10 miles north of *Titanic* and on the same side of the ice barrier, as Bisset observed, is corroborated by others aboard *Carpathia*, as well as by Captain James Moore of the *Mount Temple*. He observed *Californian* at daybreak on the 15th April, 1912, shortly after she had got underweigh, also noting that *Californian* was to the northwards of *Titanic*'s wrecksite, on the east side of the ice barrier, where *Carpathia* was now collecting *Titanic*'s lifeboats:

> JHM288: 'How near the *Carpathia* did you get that morning?'
>
> 'This pack of ice between us and the *Carpathia*, it was between 5 and 6 miles. She did not communicate with me at all. When we sighted her she must have sighted us.'
>
> JHM289: 'On which side of the ice pack was the *Californian*?'
>
> 'The *Californian* was to the north, sir. She was to the north of the *Carpathia* and steaming to the westward, because, after I had come away and after giving up my attempt to get through that pack, I came back again and steered back, thinking I might pick

up some soft place to the north. As I was going to the north the *Californian* was passing from east to west.' JHM290: 'And you were also cut off from the *Carpathia* by this ice pack?'

'Yes, sir; by this ice pack. He was then north of the *Carpathia*, and he must have been, I suppose, about the same distance to the north of the *Carpathia* as I was to the westward of her.'

Just over an hour before *Titanic's* collision, *Californian's* engines had been put into emergency reverse to bring her to a stop for the night at the edge of the ice barrier which *Titanic* so nearly reached. This action severed *Californian's* log line, causing her brass patent log to fall to the seabed. It is about a foot long and lies about 10 miles to the northwards of *Titanic's* wreck site, on a bearing of about 315° True; but exactly where and how far along that line it is would be interesting to know. Unfortunately, it is likely that this physical evidence will remain lost in the sands of time.

62 THE CALIFORNIAN SAW TITANIC'S DISTRESS SIGNALS, BUT IGNORED THEM.

Yes. The *Californian* had narrowly avoided running into the same icefield that *Titanic* would have collided with, had she not hit an outlying iceberg just before she reached the main field. Captain Lord brought *Californian* to an emergency stop just in time to avert disaster and then quite correctly decided to remain stationary until daylight. After he stopped, Lord observed *Titanic* approaching, but due to unusual atmospheric conditions, he judged her to be a 400-foot ship five miles away, instead of an 800-foot ship 10 miles away.

Thus, incorrectly convinced the ship he was looking at was not the *Titanic*, he quite correctly asked his wireless operator, Cyril Evans, to see what ships he had and to warn them about the ice. When Evans carried out this order, he discovered that the only ship within wireless range of *Californian* was the *Titanic* and informed the captain of this. Given that what Lord saw had already led him to the conclusion that the ship he was looking at was *not* the *Titanic*, this new information now led him to a second incorrect conclusion: that the ship he was looking at did not have wireless. Lord then went to bed, ordering his watch officers to therefore try to contact the stranger by Morse lamp and identify her.

The real distance between the two ships—at least 10 miles—coupled with the abnormal atmospheric conditions, meant that *Titanic* and *Californian* could not read each other's Morse signals. When his officers reported that the stranger had not replied to the Morse lamp either, this not only confirmed to Lord his impression that this was not the *Titanic*, but also convinced him that whatever ship she was must have been all right, as otherwise she would certainly have seen his signals and replied, at the distance she appeared to be.

Later that night, however, Second Officer Stone and the Apprentice, Gibson, observed several rockets in the direction of the stranger. The same abnormal atmospheric conditions also caused *Titanic*'s rockets to appear lower on the horizon, as if they could have been coming from beyond the stranger or perhaps not have been distress rockets at all. Nonetheless, Stone and Gibson correctly concluded that the ship they could see was in some sort of distress and reported this to Captain Lord.

Given that Lord believed the stranger was not the *Titanic*, had ignored his Morse and did not have wireless, he was not minded to risk his ship and the lives of his men on a wild goose chase down to this peculiar stranger in the treacherous ice conditions which had nearly sunk his own ship earlier, especially as he had no previous experience of ice and his sailing orders ordered him not to enter it. He probably concluded this was a tramp steamer with a slack crew who at worst might have broken their rudder and required assistance. Convincing himself that whatever it was could wait about three hours until daylight, when it could if necessary be dealt with quickly and safely, and reminding himself that even the international regulations concerning distress signals did not require ships to go to the aid of other ships if that meant unduly imperiling the lives of his own men, Lord took advantage of a rare opportunity for rest while his ship remained stationary.

A detailed study and explanation of the atmospheric conditions that existed at *Titanic*'s wreck site, and the part they played in the *Californian* Incident and the *Titanic* disaster, are the subject of this author's forthcoming book *A Very Deceiving Night*, further particulars of which can be found at www.averydeceivingnight.com.

63 THERE WAS A 'MYSTERY SHIP' BETWEEN THE TITANIC AND
THE CALIFORNIAN WHICH COULD HAVE SAVED EVERYONE, BUT
IT SAILED AWAY WITHOUT RESPONDING TO TITANIC'S DISTRESS
SIGNALS.

No. Apologists for Captain Lord have tried to come up with
the names of other ships in an attempt to say that these were
nearer to the *Titanic* than the *Californian*. The most famous
of these was a Norwegian sealer called the *Samson*, based on
the typescript of a journal supposedly kept by one of her
crew. According to the typescript, the original of which has
vanished, the *Samson* lay near the *Titanic*, saw the rockets,
but was engaged in illegal sealing operations and was afraid
to show herself. But unfortunately for the well-intentioned
supporters of Captain Lord, the same document puts the
Samson south of Cape Hatteras the previous afternoon.
And, as Walter Lord points out in his book, *The Night Lives
On*, 'Not even the *Mauretania*'s mighty turbines could have
propelled her to the icy waters off Newfoundland in time for
the big show.'

Furthermore, Leslie Reade, author of the brilliant book
about the *Californian* Incident, *The Ship That Stood Still*,
discovered official records in Iceland which prove that the
Samson was in the fishing port of Isafjordhur on April 6th,
1912, and then again on April 20th, 1912. She therefore
would have to have made the 3,000 mile journey to the
Titanic and back in only 14 days, which was not possible for
the 6-knot *Samson*.

In fact, the so called 'mystery ship' between the *Californian*
and the *Titanic* that night was nothing more than the result

of abnormal atmospheric conditions which made the lights of both ships appear nearer to each other than they really were. Lord tragically mistook *Titanic* for this mystery ship, which appeared to him to be a four-hundred foot ship five miles away, instead of the eight-hundred foot ship ten miles away that it really was. What they thought was the mystery ship steaming away over the horizon, was in fact *Titanic* sinking gradually into the sea.

Similarly, from *Titanic* the mystery ship appeared to sail away, despite *Californian* remaining stationary all night, but this was an illusion caused by the drifting *Californian*'s slow swinging to starboard, which made her appear from *Titanic* to be turning away. Her slow swinging to starboard eventually shut out *Californian*'s masthead light, opening her much lower stern light, which was below the horizon of those in *Titanic*'s lifeboats, thus making the so called mystery ship seem to disappear, even though *Californian*'s engines were stationary all night.

It was this same swinging motion which only revealed *Californian* to *Titanic* at about 12.20 a.m., even though *Californian* had been stationary since 10.21 p.m. that night. This is because when *Californian* first came to a stop she was heading northwards, and therefore showing *Titanic* only her low, stern light; but by about 12.20 a.m. *Californian*'s continuous slow swing to starboard had opened out her much higher masthead lights to *Titanic*, which were then noticed from the decks of the sinking liner. In reality, the mystery ship seen from the *Titanic* was the *Californian*, and the mystery ship seen from the *Californian* was the *Titanic*.

Furthermore, we can prove this. We have already seen

from *Titanic's* noon longitude that her clocks were two hours and two minutes ahead of New York Time (See question 55). We can similarly calculate from *Californian's* noon longitude of 47.25W that her clocks were one hour 50 minutes ahead of New York Time, and this was confirmed by Captain Lord:

> STL098: 'There is an hour and fifty minutes time between New York and my noon position on the 14th.'

Titanic time (at NYT+2hrs and 2mins) was therefore 12 minutes ahead of *Californian* time (at NYT+1hr and 50mins). This means that when Stone and Gibson on the *Californian* observed *Titanic's* lights disappear at 'Five minutes past two by the wheelhouse clock' (Gibson 7565), it was in fact 17 minutes past two on the *Titanic*.

Now, we know from Third Officer Pitman that *Titanic* disappeared beneath the waves at exactly 2.20am:

> HJP634: 'Can you fix the exact moment of time when the *Titanic* disappeared?'
>
> '2.20 exactly, ship's time. I took my watch out at the time she disappeared, and I said, "It is 2.20," and the passengers around me heard it.'

But we also know from the following testimony of First Class passenger Emily Ryerson and Lookout George Symonds, respectively, that *Titanic's* lights went out about three minutes before she disappeared beneath the waves:

Ryerson: 'I was in the bow of the boat with my daughter and turned to see the great ship take a plunge toward the bow, the two forward funnels seemed to lean and then she seemed to break in half as if cut with a knife, and as the bow went under the lights went out; the stern stood up for several minutes, black against the stars, and then that, too, plunged down…'

Symonds, 11512: '…and that is the time when I saw her lights go out, all her lights. The next thing I saw was her poop. As she went down like that so her poop righted itself and I thought to myself, "The poop is going to float." It could not have been more than two or three minutes after that that her poop went up as straight as anything; there was a sound like steady thunder as you hear on an ordinary night at a distance, and soon she disappeared from view.'

Therefore *Titanic*'s lights went out at 2.17 a.m., exactly when Stone and Gibson observed them go out from the bridge of the nearby *Californian*.

64 IF THE CALIFORNIAN HAD GONE TO HELP, EVERYONE ON THE TITANIC COULD HAVE BEEN SAVED.

No. Although *Californian* was only about 10 miles away, she would not have begun to move until after *Titanic's* rockets were reported to Captain Lord and he had woken up the wireless operator to get confirmation. Given that *Californian's* Second Officer, Herbert Stone, first observed *Titanic's* rockets at 1.10 a.m., and even assuming they had ignored the incorrect distress position given by *Titanic* and gone instead in the direction of the rockets they could see, *Californian* would not have been underway before 1.20 a.m., or about an hour before *Titanic* sank. Given that *Californian's* top speed was 14 knots, this means she could have arrived only as *Titanic* was preparing for her final plunge.

Californian would have had to stand off the sinking Titanic at this stage and would therefore only have been able to haul people out of the water. Given the sub-zero temperature of the water at *Titanic's* wrecksite, this would have met with limited success and those she did manage to save would probably not have been more than those who were in *Titanic's* lifeboats anyway, as many of these people would not have taken to the lifeboats if they had clearly seen a rescue ship on its way.

This is a far cry from Senator Smith's conclusion to the American Enquiry that:

'Had [Captain Lord] been as vigilant in the movement of his vessel as he was active in displaying his own signal lamp, there is a very strong probability that every human life that was sacrificed through this disaster could have been saved.'

And Lord Mersey's judgment in the British Enquiry:

'The night was clear and the sea was smooth. When she first saw the rockets the *Californian* could have pushed through the ice to the open water without any serious risk and so have come to the assistance of the *Titanic*. Had she done so she might have saved many if not all of the lives that were lost.'

Women and Children First

65 CAPTAIN SMITH HAD A MENTAL BREAKDOWN FOLLOWING THE COLLISION, WHICH RENDERED HIM INEFFECTIVE.

No, although Captain Smith suddenly found himself in an impossible and overwhelming situation, which must have been unbelievable to the 62-year-old captain, who had captained 17 White Star vessels, and who in 1907 told the New York press:

> 'When anyone asks me how I can best describe my experiences of nearly 40 years at sea, I merely say "uneventful". I have never been in an accident of any sort worth speaking about. I never saw a wreck and have never been wrecked, nor was I ever in any predicament that threatened to end in disaster of any sort.'

Titanic's evacuation was characterized by poor organization, although this was largely due to Captain Smith knowing that there were only lifeboats for about half of those on board and wanting to avoid a panic. He therefore decided not to communicate the gravity of the situation, even to all his officers; although he did tell them the truth if they asked him

Tim Maltin

directly, as Fourth Officer Boxhall did about half an hour after the collision:

> 15610: 'Did you hear the Captain say anything to anybody about the ship being doomed?'
>
> 'The Captain did remark something to me in the earlier part of the evening after the order had been given to clear the boats. I encountered him when reporting something to him, or something, and he was inquiring about the men going on with the work, and I said, "Yes, they are carrying on all right." I said, "Is it really serious?" He said, "Mr. Andrews tells me he gives her from an hour to an hour and a half."'

Smith's deliberate lack of communication about the gravity of the situation, combined with the fact that the crew was new to the ship and that *Titanic* had never had a full lifeboat drill, caused confusion, but not panic.

The myth of Smith having some sort of a breakdown, though, probably stems from the fact that Lightoller had to ask the Captain if it was alright to load the lifeboats with women and children:

> CHL514: (Senator SMITH) 'You asked the captain on the boat deck whether the lifeboats should take the women and children first, if I understand you correctly?'
> Mr. LIGHTOLLER: 'Not quite, sir; I asked him: "Shall I put the women and children in the boats?" The captain replied, "Yes, and lower away."'

However, this delay was probably caused only by the deafening noise of the steam escaping from *Titanic's* boilers, which made giving orders on the boat deck impossible and caused Lightoller to resort to hand signals:

> 13797: 'You were just telling us what you found when you came up on deck after you had heard of what had happened, and I think you just told us that the steam was roaring off—blowing out of the boilers, I suppose?
> 'Yes.'
> 13798: 'Was it making a great noise?'
> 'Yes.'
> 13799: 'So great as to be difficult to hear what was said?'
> 'Very difficult.'
> 13811: 'Had you any means of knowing what boat a particular seaman would be attached to if he did not know; have you any means of telling him?'
> 'Well, I did not think it advisable, taking into consideration the row going on with the steam to make any inquiries. I could only direct them by motions of the hand. They could not hear what I said.'

Lightoller was in fact asking Captain Smith to adjudicate when he felt that *Titanic's* Chief Officer, Henry Tingle Wilde was being too slow and cautious about swinging out the boats:

> 13820: 'And what did Mr. Wilde say about that—

what were the orders?'

'I am under the impression that Mr. Wilde said "No," or "Wait," something to that effect, and meeting the Commander, I asked him, and he said, "Yes, swing out."'

In the following similar testimony from Third Officer Pitman it seems as though *Titanic*'s owner, Bruce Ismay, was taking the lead over Captain Smith in organising the evacuation, although this was probably also because the noise of escaping steam was making it hard to communicate orders on the Boat Deck at this time:

HJP816: 'As I understand, you say that Mr. Ismay told you that you had better get aboard with the women and children?'

'No, no. He remarked to me, "You had better go ahead and get the women and children"; and I replied that I would await the commander's orders. I did not know it was Mr. Ismay at the time.'

HJP817: 'Did you tell him what Mr. Ismay said?'

'I said I judged that it was Mr. Ismay.'

HJP818: 'And you told him what Mr. Ismay said?'

'Yes.'

HJP819: 'What did the commander say?'

'Carry on.'

Captain Smith apparently made a simple mistake in the following testimony of First Class passenger Hugh Woolner:

HUW019: 'Did you have occasion to see the captain occasionally?'

'I asked somebody to point him out to me. Naturally, one is interested to know the appearance of the captain, and I knew him by sight.'

HUW021: 'Did you see him the night of the accident?'

'Not until I came up onto the boat deck, and he was there on the port side.'

HUW025: 'How long was this after the collision?'

'I did not look at my watch, but I should think it was half an hour.'

HUW026: 'Did you hear him say anything or did you say anything to him?'

'Yes; I did. I made one remark to him. He said: "I want all the passengers to go down on A deck, because I intend they shall go into the boats from A deck." I remembered noticing as I came up that all those glass windows were raised to the very top; and I went up to the captain and saluted him and said: "Haven't you forgotten, sir, that all those glass windows are closed?" He said: "By God, you are right. Call those peopleback." Very few people had moved, but the few that had gone down the companionway came up again, and everything went on all right.'

But even if this was indeed Captain Smith, as Woolner thought it was, this small mistake is understandable, especially given Smith's familiarity with *Titanic*'s nearly identical sister, whose promenade deck was open at this point. However, it is possible that Hugh Woolner was confusing Captain Smith with Lightoller in this incident, or that Lightoller made the same mistake, as Lightoller clearly attributes this mistake to himself:

13834: (The Commissioner) 'That is what I want to know?'

'Well, you see, if I may give it to you in the order that I was working, I swung out No. 4 with the intention of loading all the boats from A deck, the next deck below the boat deck. I lowered No. 4 down to A deck, and gave orders for the women and children to go down to A deck to be loaded through the windows. My reason for loading the boats through the windows from A deck was that there was a coaling wire, a very strong wire running along A deck, and I thought it would be very useful to trice the boat to in case the ship got a slight list or anything; but as I was going down the ladder after giving the order, someone sung out and said the windows were up. I countermanded the order and told the people to come back on the boat deck and instructed two or three, I think they were stewards, to find the handles and lower the windows. That left No. 4 boat hanging at A deck, so then I went on to No. 6.'

In any event, we know from the following testimony from Major Arthur Peuchen that Smith did not make that mistake again:

AGP076: 'The captain was standing still by him [Lightoller] at that time, and I think, although the officer ordered me to the boat, the captain said, "You had better go down below and break a window and get in through a window, into the boat"…although Major Peuchen did not regard the Captain's suggestion as feasible.'

AGP077: 'The captain said that?'

'Yes. That was his suggestion; and I said I did not think it was feasible, and I said I could get in the boat if I could get hold of a rope. However, we got hold of a loose rope in some way that was hanging from the davit, near the block anyway, and by getting hold of it I swung myself off the ship, and lowered myself into the boat.'

AGP078: 'How far did you have to swing yourself?'

'The danger was jumping off from the boat. It was not after I got a straight line; it was very easy lowering.'

However, it seems that Captain Smith was simply doing his best to assist:

AGP107: 'From what you saw of the captain, was he alert and watchful?'

'He was doing everything in his power to get women in these boats, and to see that they were lowered properly. I thought he was doing his duty in regard to the lowering of the boats, sir.'

And Captain Smith continued to do his best under the terrible circumstances and to give orders, right until the very end, with no signs that he had suffered any kind of breakdown. Surviving Marconi operator Harold Bride said that a few minutes before *Titanic* began her final plunge, Captain Smith went to the Marconi operators' room and released them from their duties:

> 'Just at this moment the captain came into the cabin and said, "You can do nothing more; look out for yourselves."'

And Smith was still busy releasing *Titanic*'s crew from their duties a few minutes later, when *Titanic*'s decks were actually awash, as Steward Edward Brown remembered:

> 10585: 'The Captain came past us while we were trying to get this boat away with a megaphone in his hand, and he spoke to us.'
> 10586: 'What did he say?'
> 'He said, "Well, boys, do your best for the women and children, and look out for yourselves." He walked on the bridge.'

66 TITANIC'S PASSENGERS WERE RELUCTANT TO GET INTO THE LIFEBOATS.

Yes. In an attempt to avoid a panic, passengers and crew had not been told of the full gravity of the situation, only that they must put on lifejackets and that the women and children must go away in the lifeboats, as a precaution. Most people believed that *Titanic* would either not sink, or that she would only sink after several hours, by which time they believed a fleet of rescue ships would have come to their aid, having received *Titanic*'s wireless distress signals. Certainly, the bright decks of the largest liner in the world seemed more secure than a rowing boat on a dark night in the middle of the North Atlantic.

When the first boat was being loaded, lifeboat number 7, on the starboard side of the ship, outside *Titanic*'s First Class entrance, First Officer Murdoch requested: 'Any passengers who would like to do so may get into this lifeboat,' but only a trickle of passengers came forward. This lifeboat had a capacity of 65 persons, but was eventually lowered at 12.40 a.m., an hour after *Titanic*'s collision, with only 28 people in it.

As well as being frightened of being lowered 70 feet down the side of *Titanic* on a freezing night, many women understandably did not want to leave their husbands or the perceived safety of *Titanic*.

It is telling that, climbing *Titanic*'s grand staircase to the Boat Deck, First Class passenger Mrs Helen Churchill Candee, travelling alone, entrusted the care of her most cherished possession—an ivory and gold miniature of her mother—to a shipboard friend, Mr Edward A. Kent, presumably thinking it would be safer with him, than with her in an open boat. When Kent's body was recovered, the miniature was still in his jacket pocket and was returned safely to Mrs Candee.

67 TITANIC'S OFFICERS THOUGHT HER LIFEBOATS MIGHT BREAK IF THEY WERE LOWERED FULLY LOADED.

Yes. *Titanic*'s boats had been inspected on 30th May, 1911, by William H. Chantler, a ship Surveyor in the Marine Department of the Board of Trade, stationed at Belfast, and found fit to carry 70 persons:

24038: 'On the 19th May, 1911, did you receive special instructions to look closely into the construction of all new boats?'

'From the Board of Trade, yes.'

24039: 'That was the 19th May, 1911?'

'Yes, the 19th May, 1911.'

24040: 'Did you begin to inspect the *Titanic*'s boats on the 30th May, 1911?'

'Yes.'

24041: 'After this?'

'Yes, ten days after.'

24042: 'Did you inspect them carefully?'

'Yes.'

24043: 'Fourteen lifeboats and the two other boats?'

'There were 14 section A boats and two of section D.'

24044: 'Were they well made and of good material?'

'They were well made and of good material.'

24045: 'Would they be safe to lower from the davits full of passengers?'

'I made a calculation and came to the conclusion that they would be.'

24046: 'Now, what is the full capacity of those boats?'

'I think it was 618 cubic feet.'

24047: 'How many people ought to be lowered in one of these lifeboats?'

'Under the statutory Rules they should carry 65.'

24048: 'The boats that you saw, how many people would they take safely from the davits, in your judgment?'

'Well, as many as the statutory Rules would allow.'

24049: 'How many; cannot you give me a number; it would save a lot of time?'

'A matter of 70.'

The *Olympic* Class lifeboats had also been tested by her builders, Harland & Wolff, on 9th May, 1911. At this test, one of *Olympic*'s lifeboats had been loaded with weights equivalent to a full compliment of 65 persons and successfully lowered up and down six times, without any sign of strain. However, neither Captain Smith nor any of *Titanic*'s officers seems to have been made aware of these tests, as Third Officer Pitman testified at the US Inquiry:

HJP834: 'Do I correctly understand you to say that you would not consider it safe to load a boat to its full capacity at the rail before lowering it?'

'No; I do not think it would be wise to do it.'

It is tragic that for this erroneous reason, *Titanic*'s most senior surviving officer, Charles Herbert Lightoller, chose to only half-fill *Titanic*'s lifeboats with women and children from the deck, with the intention of filling them with men later, when the boats were on the water; and because he had not been made aware of the speed with which *Titanic* would sink, he never had time to fill them completely:

14491: (The Commissioner) 'There are two or three matters about the boats I should like to ask a question on. (To the witness.) I want to know whether you knew that those boats were not intended to be lowered full of people. Did you know that?'

'We have no instructions to that effect, My Lord, but I knew that it was not practicable to lower them full of people.'

14492: 'Had you any reason to suppose that they were weaker than they should have been?'

'No. I have not had much experience with these Englehardt collapsible boats.'

14493: 'I am not talking about collapsible boats merely, but the lifeboats?'

'I should not think they were capable of being lowered full of people. They may be. I have never seen them full of people, but if they are only supposed to carry 65 people afloat, it hardly seems feasible that they would carry 65 people when suspended at each end. It does not seem seamanlike to fill a boat chock full of people when it is only suspended at each end. It is to guard principally against accidents in lowering. That must be taken into consideration a very great deal—the fact that you have to lower a boat from a great height and get her safely into the water. It is of more importance to get the boat into the water than it is to actually fill her at the boat deck, because it is no use filling her if you are going to lose those people before you get her down; it is far better to save a few and safely.'

14494: (Mr. Scanlan.) 'Do you think you could have filled the boat still more in the water?'

'Undoubtedly.'

14495: 'If your organisation had been complete?'

'I do not see the organisation would have prevented the ship sinking.'

14496: 'I know it would not?'

'It was that that prevented us putting the people in.'

In fact, *Titanic*'s lifeboats could have taken a weight equivalent to 130 people, suspended from both ends in the davits, as further tests to this type of lifeboat, carried out by Mr Chantler after the disaster, proved:

24052: (Mr. Rowlatt, to the witness) 'Have you made a calculation to find what strain the boats would bear in being lowered?'

'Yes, I made such a calculation. The results I arrived at were that the stress at the gunwale would be 2 cwts. to the square inch, and at the keel about 2 1/4 cwts.'

24053: 'When did you make that calculation?'

'After the casualty occurred.'

24054: 'Is that more than the stress which would be brought to bear by the boat being lowered with 70 people in it?'

'That is the stress that would be brought to bear with 65 persons in the boat, and with the boat suspended from the davits, not water-borne.'

24055: 'Do you say that you made a calculation that shows the boat would stand a greater stress than that produced by the people being in it or not?'

'The result of my calculation was that—'

24056: 'That it would bear a greater stress?'

'That it would bear a greater stress.'

24057: 'Much greater?'

'Considerably greater.'

24058: 'Can you give us a percentage?'

'Twice as much.'

68 TITANIC'S SECOND OFFICER PREVENTED MEN AND EVEN BOYS FROM ENTERING LIFEBOATS EVEN THOUGH THERE WAS SPACE FOR THEM.

Yes, almost certainly because of his views about loading the lifeboats from the water, explained above. Lightoller tried to prevent 13-year-old John Ryerson from entering lifeboat no.4 before his father successfully argued that at 13 he was young enough to count as a 'child' and go with his mother —although in 1912 John was legally able, had he wanted, to leave school aged 12 and enter the workforce. The story goes that Lightoller then allowed the young John Ryerson in, grumbling 'No more Boys.'

Lightoller also famously refused entry to Colonel John Jacob Astor IV, the richest man in the world in 1912, who asked to go with his pregnant wife Madeleine. Lifeboat 4 was eventually lowered at 1.55 a.m. with around 36 people in it, only about half its total capacity. Lightoller knew that speed was of the essence and, although he waited for more women for 10 minutes after the Astors had arrived, he could not wait any longer than that as *Titanic* was now listing heavily and sinking fast.

Lightoller was a notorious 'hard case' who had already been ship-wrecked in 1889 at the age of 16 when the *Holt Hill*, a four-masted barque and three skysail-yarder, ran aground in a storm on the four-and-a-half-square-mile uninhabited island of St Paul's in the middle of the South Indian Ocean, 3,000 miles east of The Cape of Good Hope. He and the other surviving crew members were only rescued eight days later when a passing ship, the *Coorong*, saw the smoke from their fire and took them to Adelaide, where they arrived 22 days later. Lightoller also knew all about surviving in the cold, having spent a desperate year in 1898 prospecting for gold in the Yukon, in Canada's frozen North-West, in temperatures often as low as -40° C.

Although Lightoller will always be criticised for not allowing more men into the lifeboats he launched, it should be noted that 193 women were saved from the port side of *Titanic*, where he was working, as opposed to only 154 women saved from the starboard side, where First Officer Murdoch worked all night.

69 ONE MAN ESCAPED BY PRETENDING TO BE A WOMAN IN ORDER TO GET INTO A LIFEBOAT.

Yes, and it is possible that more than one man might have done so. Fifth Officer Lowe said that he had discovered a man dressed as a woman when he was transferring passengers out of no.14 into other boats preparatory to going back to pick up more people:

> HGL624: 'Then I asked for volunteers to go with me to the wreck, and it was at this time that I found this Italian. He came aft, and he had a shawl over his head and I suppose he had skirts. Anyhow, I pulled this shawl off his face and saw he was a man. He was in a great hurry to get into the other boat, and I caught hold of him and pitched him in.'

In fact, this was probably Third Class passenger Edward Ryan, who freely admitted in a letter to his parents that he had put a towel over his head in order to pass as a woman and enter a lifeboat. He was Irish, but Lowe may not have realised this in the dark, and probably allowed his prejudices about foreigners in general and Italians in particular to colour his judgment of the man's true nationality.

Lifeboat 4 also attracted a female disguise story. 11-year-old William Carter, Jr, was apparently being prevented from entering it, so William's mother put a woman's hat on his head and bundled him into the boat with her. In fact, William himself said that he did not wear a hat into the boat; Mrs Carter put the hat on his head when they were already in the lifeboat and had left the ship, in an effort to keep him warm. When lifeboat no.4 came alongside *Carpathia* the next morning, William Carter Sr, who had been rescued in another boat and was already on board, could not see his son until William Jr swept the hat off and called up, 'Here I am, Father.' The *Worcester Evening Gazette* of 19th April, 1912, later embellished this story with a different cast of characters, claiming that the incident had involved Madeleine Astor putting a hat on John Ryerson's head and declaring, 'Now he's a girl, so he can go.'

Third Class passenger Daniel Buckley thought that Mrs Astor had thrown her shawl over him as a disguise when she found him hiding in the bottom of her lifeboat, number 4. Whoever did help Daniel Buckley, it was not Madeleine Astor as he was in Boat 4, whereas Buckley was in Boat 13.

But some of these female disguise stories were entirely fictional. William Sloper, a stockbroker in First Class, was accused of escaping in this way, but he left *Titanic* in lifeboat number 7, the first one to be launched. First Officer Murdoch allowed both men and women into this lifeboat, so Sloper had no reason to disguise himself as a woman, and in fact the story was published in the *New York Herald*, one of William Randolph Hearst's newspapers, apparently as revenge for his refusing to talk to their reporter and instead giving the exclusive on his *Titanic* story to his friend at the *New Britain Herald*. On the advice of his family and friends, Sloper refrained from bringing an action for libel.

70 TITANIC DEVELOPED A LIST TO PORT WHEN SINKING AND PASSENGERS WERE ORDERED TO THE STARBOARD SIDE TO CORRECT IT.

Yes. *Titanic* carried a permanent, but slight, list to port on her maiden voyage, caused by the loading of the ship. However, immediately after the collision, which was on her starboard side, she listed to starboard, as the initial water rushed in. Passenger Norman Chambers noticed both *Titanic*'s permanent list to port and her list to starboard immediately following the collision:

> NCC005: 'However, there was then a noticeable list to starboard, with probably a few degrees of pitch; and as the ship had a list to port nearly all afternoon, I decided to remain up, in spite of a feeling of perfect safety.'

This initial list to starboard immediately after the collision was caused by water from the breaches in *Titanic*'s hull initially being trapped on the starboard side of the previously watertight firemen's passage, which ran longitudinally down the centre of the forward part of the hull.

However, as water continued to pour into the hull, its pressure began to equalise across *Titanic's* keel. This allowed her permanent list to port to be restored and then exaggerated by the water which continued to rush in, as Colonel Archibald Gracie recalled in his 1912 account, *The Truth about the Titanic*:

> 'When we were loading the last boat, just a short time before it was fully loaded, a palpable list toward the port side began, and the officer called out, "All passengers to the starboard side," and Smith [his friend Clinch-Smith] and myself went to the starboard side, still at the bow of the ship.'

It may seem that the order to move men around *Titanic* in an attempt to keep her on an even keel was an odd one, given the ship's great weight. However, because *Titanic* was now lying on her rounded bilge keel, and not the much flatter central keel on which she was designed to float, the shape of her hull made her 'tender', and thus it was possible to affect the list to some extent by moving people around. The number of people required to make a significant difference, however, was more than were available; one of the *Titanic* designers, Edward Wilding, estimated that moving 800 people 50 feet would only have corrected the list by about 2 degrees—not much when the ship was listing by as much as 10 degrees.

71 TITANIC'S FIRST OFFICER ALLOWED A LIFEBOAT WITH A CAPACITY OF 40 TO LEAVE WITH ONLY FIVE PASSENGERS IN IT.

Yes. First Officer Murdoch, loading lifeboats on *Titanic*'s starboard side, allowed men into lifeboats as long as there was space left and no women or children were waiting in the immediate vicinity. Therefore, when the Duff Gordons asked him if they might enter *Titanic*'s emergency lifeboat No. 1, he agreed. Even so, this boat was lowered with only 12 people in it, mostly men, and only five of whom were passengers. This was because most passengers on that part of the deck had already left by lifeboats 7, 5 and 3. Indeed, the previous lifeboat, No. 3, had been sent away with about 10 Firemen in it, because no more passengers were nearby who were willing to go. Murdoch needed to get emergency boat No. 1 away quickly in order to have enough time to first launch *Titanic*'s starboard stern boats, and then launch Collapsible A down the same falls as Boat No. 1, particularly in view of the alarming list to port which *Titanic* was developing at this time, and which threatened to make further launching of the starboard boats impossible. Despite his haste, Murdoch still did not succeed in launching Collapsible A before it was washed off the deck in *Titanic*'s final moments.

Like all the officers, Murdoch was racing against time to get all the lifeboats launched before the ship sank, even if it meant leaving some with places in them. Hindsight is a wonderful luxury to have, and Murdoch worked under almost unbearable stress to get *Titanic*'s lifeboats away, despite his being fully aware of the ship's grave condition, as testified by Third Officer Herbert Pitman, whom Murdoch ordered away in only the second lifeboat to leave the *Titanic*, at 12.45 a.m.:

> 15034: (Mr. Butler Aspinall) 'Did Mr. Murdoch, in addition to telling you to keep handy to come back to the gangway, say anything more to you?'
> 'No; he only shook hands and said, "Good-bye, good luck"; that was all.'
> 15035: 'When he said "Good-bye" to you in that way, did you think the situation was serious; did you think the ship was doomed then?'
> 'I did not, but I thought he must have thought so.'

Similarly, *Titanic*'s Chief Second Class steward, John Hardy, testified at the US Inquiry:

> JOH063: 'People even then thought she would float?'
> 'Of course I had great respect and great regard for Chief Officer Murdoch, and I was walking along the deck forward with him, and he said, "I believe she is gone, Hardy"; and that is the only time I thought she might sink; when he said that.'

In fact, 386 people were saved from the starboard side, where First Officer Murdoch worked almost exclusively all night, whereas only 279 people were saved from the port side.

72 THIRD CLASS PASSENGERS WERE KEPT BELOW AS TITANIC SANK AND WERE PREVENTED FROM ENTERING THE LIFEBOATS.

No, but this is possibly true in the case of some Third Class men, in some parts of the ship, who were not allowed up to the lifeboats with the women and children under the rule of Women and Children first. It is a myth that Third Class passengers, including women and children, were locked below until the end. This idea stems from the fact that the order to pass the Third Class women and children up to the boats was not given until 12.30 a.m., 50 minutes after the collision. However, *Titanic*'s first lifeboat, No. 7, was not launched until after this time, at 12.40 a.m. Third Class passenger Daniel Buckley was one of those men who was allowed up to the lifeboats, but he describes the alarming wait beforehand, while the boats were being got ready and swung out, prior to loading at 12.30 a.m:

> DAB016: 'Was there any effort made on the part of the officers or crew to hold the steerage passengers in the steerage?'
> 'I do not think so.'
> DAB017: 'Were you permitted to go on up to the top deck without any interference?'
> 'Yes, sir. They tried to keep us down at first on our steerage deck. They did not want us to go up to the first class place at all.'
> DAB018: 'Who tried to do that?'
> 'I can not say who they were. I think they were sailors.'

DAB019: 'What happened then? Did the steerage passengers try to get out?'

'Yes; they did. There was one steerage passenger there, and he was getting up the steps, and just as he was going in a little gate a fellow came along and chucked him down; threw him down into the steerage place. This fellow got excited, and he ran after him, and he could not find him. He got up over the little gate. He did not find him.'

DAB020: 'What gate do you mean?'

'A little gate just at the top of the stairs going up into the first class deck.'

DAB021: 'There was a gate between the steerage and the first class deck?'

'Yes. The first class deck was higher up than the steerage deck, and there were some steps leading up to it; 9 or 10 steps, and a gate just at the top of the steps.'

DAB022: 'Was the gate locked?'

'It was not locked at the time we made the attempt to get up there, but the sailor, or whoever he was, locked it. So that this fellow that went up after him broke the lock on it, and he went after the fellow that threw him down. He said if he could get hold of him he would throw him into the ocean.'

DAB023: 'Did these passengers in the steerage have any opportunity at all of getting out?'

'Yes; they had.'

DAB024: 'What opportunity did they have?'

'I think they had as much chance as the first and

second class passengers.'
DAB025: 'After this gate was broken?'

'Yes; because they were all mixed. All the steerage passengers went up on the first class deck at this time, when the gate was broken. They all got up there. They could not keep them down.'

After 12.30 a.m. all Third Class women and children passengers were assisted to the boat deck and stewards were positioned throughout Third Class to direct passengers to the lifeboats.

The doors and gates, including the one which Buckley refers to above, between Third Class and the rest of the ship were normally kept closed to comply with 1912 immigration laws. These required physical separation between Third Class and the other classes to help prevent the spread of infectious diseases. However, Third Class Steward John Hart testified that all these gates and doors were opened at 12.30 a.m:

10151: (Hart) 'I should like to know what are the means employed to prevent the third class passengers during the voyage from straying into the first and second class decks and quarters of the ship. First, are there collapsible gates?'

'Yes, gates that can be removed. Dividing the third class deck there is a companion; dividing the second class deck and the first class deck there is a barrier.'
10152: 'Are those kept fastened during the course of a voyage - the barrier and the companion?'

'No.'

10153: 'Are they open?'

'Well, the barrier that lifts over and the gate that fixes in, you can just take it out with your hand; it is never locked.'

10154: 'Do I understand you to say that those gates are not locked at any time and the barrier is not fastened?'

'Not to my knowledge.'

10155: 'So that at any time a third class passenger, by pushing the gate or by raising the barrier, can go to the second class deck or to the first class deck. Is that right?'

'That is correct. That is, of course, if there is nobody there on watch. There usually is a quartermaster standing by there or a seaman.'

10156: 'Have you ever seen those gates locked?'

'No, I was not long enough on the ship to see them locked.'

10165: 'You did not look whether the gates were locked or the barrier closed from the time you went on to the *Titanic* until the time of the accident. Is that so?'

'I do not see how they could be locked. I do not think so at all.'

10170: (The Commissioner) 'They were all down, as I understand, when you were bringing the passengers away?'

'Yes, My Lord.'

10171: 'All three were opened?'

'Yes, My Lord.'

10172: (Mr. Harbinson): 'Did you see anybody open these gates or raise these barriers?'

'No, I did not see anybody open them; but I had to pass through them, and I saw them open.'

10213: 'You have told us that you saw a number of stewards placed at various portions to direct the third class passengers how they were to go?'

'Yes.'

10214: 'About how many stewards were so placed?'

'I passed about five or six on the starboard side.'

10215: 'Who else besides you, then, were bringing the people from their berths—rousing them and bringing them up to the boat deck? How many others?'

'Almost eight. A portion of the third class stewards were room stewards, of whom I am the only survivor.'

10216: 'I understood that there were only eight third class stewards in the aft portion altogether?'

'To look after them.'

10217: 'Who were stationed at various places to direct the third class passengers the way they were to go?'

'Not of that eight.'

10218: 'There were five?'

'Five others.'

10219: 'What class stewards were they?'

'I could not tell you. Stewards were placed all round the ship.'

10220: 'Do you know who placed them there?'

'I cannot tell you.'

10221: 'Do you know the stewards by sight who were

placed to direct the third class passengers?'

'No.'

10222: 'But you say they were not third class stewards?'

'They were not third class stewards.'

10223: 'Did you see the emergency door open?'

'I saw it open—The swing door to the second class you mean?'

10224: 'Yes?'

'Yes.'

10225: 'Do you know at what time it was opened?'

'Yes, I can tell you. It was open at half-past 12.'

10230: (The Commissioner) 'Did you see anyone keeping the third class passengers back, so as to prevent them getting to the boat deck?'

'No, My Lord.'

10255: 'According to you, all the women and children, from the aft part of the boat who were taken up and who wanted to escape could have done so?'

'I do not doubt that for a moment.'

10317: 'When you returned from your first visit to the boat deck you told us you had some trouble to get back owing to the men trying to get up. What prevented you?'

'**The stewards prevented these men getting up when the order was passed around for the women and children**.' [Author's emphasis]

10322: 'I suppose you found they got a little excited when they were asked to put their lifebelts on?'

'They were simply told to put their lifebelts on in

a quiet manner to prevent any kind of a panic that might have ensued.'

10323: And you did your best to discharge that duty?'

'Yes.'

10324: 'Was that before any order had been passed along that these people were to go up to the boat deck?'

'Yes.'

10325: 'And when the order was passed along that they were to be taken up to the boat deck, did you do your best to get them through?'

'I did my duty, Sir, to get them through.'

Third Class men in some areas of the ship were required to wait below, under the rule of women and children first; and although there were no physical barriers preventing Third Class women and children passengers from reaching the boats, and stewards were guiding them to the boat deck, Steward Hart also recalls that many women in Third Class were unwilling to go to the lifeboats. Some went to the boat deck but found it too cold, some felt it was safer to stay on the ship than to get into a small rowing boat in the middle of the Atlantic on a dark night, and some did not want to leave their husbands:

9921: 'Now just tell us about the next thing?'

'I was standing by waiting for further instructions. After some little while the word came down, "Pass your women up on the boat deck." This was done.'

9922: 'That means the third class?'

'Yes, the third class.'

9923: 'Anything about children?'

'Yes. "Pass the women and children."'

9924: '"Pass the women and children up to the boat deck"?'

'Yes, those that were willing to go to the boat deck were shown the way. Some were not willing to go to the boat deck, and stayed behind. Some of them went to the boat deck, and found it rather cold, and saw the boats being lowered away, and thought themselves more secure on the ship, and consequently returned to their cabin.'

9925: 'You say they thought themselves more secure on the ship? Did you hear any of them say so?'

'Yes, I heard two or three say they preferred to remain on the ship than be tossed about on the water like a cockle shell.'

9926: 'Can you in any way help us to fix the time, or about the time, when the order was given to pass the third class women and children up to the boat deck? Could you tell us how long it was after you were first roused, or how long it was before the ship went down?'

'Well, as near as I can. The vessel struck, I believe, at 11.40. That would be 20 minutes to 12. It must have been three parts of an hour before the word was passed down to me to pass the women and children up to the boat deck.'

9927 (The Commissioner) 'This would be about 12.30?'

'Yes, My Lord, as near as can be.'

10076: 'Lord Mersey has just pointed out that you told us, on the boat deck where the boat left there were some women and their husbands. How was it they did not get into the boats?'

'Because the cry was for the women and children, and the boat at that time was practically full of women and children, and these women would not leave their husbands.'

10077: 'That is what I wanted, that was the impression you got, was it?'

'Yes.'

10078: 'Did you hear any of them say so on the boat deck?'

'Yes.'

10079: 'You did?'

'Yes.'

10080: 'You have told us that you were one of a number of some 60 third class stewards?'

'Yes.'

10081: 'Can you tell me how many third class stewards were saved?'

'Yes, I believe 11 or 12.'

10082: 'Out of 60?'

'Yes.'

Examined by Mr. SCANLAN.

10096: 'At first, I take it, you were trying to assure the passengers under your charge that they were in safety?'

'Yes.'

10097: 'When you realised that the position was very serious, what did you say to those people?'

'I told the people to lose no time in getting to the boat deck.'

10098: 'Did you tell them the ship was sinking?'

'No, I did not know the ship was sinking.'

10099: 'Even amongst the 49 women and children for whom you were responsible, did some of those go back to their quarters?'

'Yes.'

10100: 'And refused to go?'

'Yes.'

10101: 'When those people refused to go, did you again go back to them and tell them that those in charge knew that the ship was in a very dangerous condition?'

'Yes; they were informed the second time I went back.'

10102: 'You made it perfectly clear to them?'

'Everything was clear.'

10193: 'How many women refused to leave their berths?'

'Several.'

Nor was there any discrimination against third Class women and children on the boat deck, as Fifth Officer Lowe explained at the US Inquiry:

HGL487: 'What did you do about it yourself? Did you arbitrarily select from the deck?'

'You say "select." There was no such thing as selecting. It was simply the first woman, whether first class, second class, third class, or sixty-seventh class. It was all the same; women and children were first.'

HGL488: 'You mean that there was a procession of women—'

'The first woman was first into the boat, and the second woman was second into the boat, no matter whether she was a first class passenger or any other class.'

Nevertheless, most Third Class passengers only occupied *Titanic's* stern-most and forward-most lifeboats in any numbers, and this was probably because these were nearer to the Third Class areas, there being no lifeboats at all stationed in third class areas of the ship.

Having listened to all the evidence at the British Inquiry, Mr Harbinson, the lawyer appointed to act for the Third Class passengers, concluded that there was no evidence of active discrimination against Third Class in the evacuation:

'Now, my Lord, I wish to say distinctly that no evidence has been given in the course of this case that would substantiate a charge that any attempt was made to keep back the third class passengers. I desire further, my Lord, to say that there is no evidence that when they did reach the boat deck there was any discrimination practised either by the Officers or the sailors in putting them into the boats. It would be wrong of me to say so, because there is no evidence which would bear me out in saying so, and I think it only fair that in speaking on behalf of the third class passengers I should make that observation to your Lordship.'

Harbinson thought that much of the reason why a smaller percentage of Third Class women and children were saved than First and Second Class women and children stemmed from a lack of guidance for Third Class passengers. Despite Hart's evidence, Harbinson thought that the organisation of stewards to take Third Class up to the boat deck could have been greatly improved, especially given that many in Third Class would be unused to travelling on ships and would find it hard to make their way to the boat deck. He also thought that passengers ought to have been informed that the ship was sinking by some general alarm, which he said, despite suggestions that this would have caused a panic, was something they had a right to know and would have given them a better sense of the need to get to the boat deck as quickly as possible.

No-one can argue with these sentiments; and the fact that lifeboats went away with empty places in them, when elsewhere on the ship others wished to fill those places, can only be put down to poor organization, despite the need to avoid a panic.

No third class passengers were called to give evidence at the British Inquiry and only three gave evidence in the US, but even these three testified that they had not been discriminated against.

It is likely that they understood that the rule of women

and children first applied to all classes and they were aware that Third Class women and children were invited to go up to the boat deck as soon as the lifeboats were ready for lowering. Nonetheless, and despite the harshness of the situation that the lack of lifeboats created, the thought that some men were required to remain below until very near the end is saddening and shocking.

Although they were in a sense crew, and therefore not strictly relevant to this discussion, we know that all the staff from the Ritz restaurant concession on the *Titanic* were kept below. As a result, all of them died except for the Head Chef's secretary, Paul Maugé, who was also the maître d' of the restaurant. However, M. Maugé said that he thought he and the chef, Pierre Rousseau, had been allowed onto the boat deck only because they were dressed as passengers, whereas the other staff were in their working dress and were therefore seen as crew and ordered to remain on *Titanic's* stern well deck, where there were no lifeboats, until all the lifeboats had gone.

As *Titanic* began to break up and sink rapidly after all her lifeboats had been launched, many passengers who had remained or been kept below suddenly poured out onto the Boat Deck, as described by *Titanic* survivor Colonel Archibald Gracie, in his detailed 1912 account of the sinking, *The Truth About The Titanic*:

'My friend Clinch Smith made the proposition that we should leave and go toward the stern. But there arose before us from the decks below a mass of humanity several lines deep converging on the Boat

Deck facing us and completely blocking our passage to the stern. There were women in the crowd as well as men and these seemed to be steerage passengers who had just come up from the decks below. Even among these people there was no hysterical cry, no evidence of panic. Oh the agony of it.'

73 IF TITANIC HAD HAD MORE LIFEBOATS, EVERYBODY COULD HAVE BEEN SAVED.

No. *Titanic* already carried enough lifeboats for all of the 534 women and children on board and more than an equal number of men, as her lifeboat capacity was 1,178. Yet only 711 people survived the disaster and 50 of these were saved (or saved themselves) from the water (or by jumping into lifeboats as they were being lowered). In fact *Titanic's* officers only managed to launch two of the four collapsible lifeboats which *Titanic* carried, and these had a capacity of 47 people each. Moreover, the 18 lifeboats they did launch left the ship only two-thirds full, with enough space left in them to save 423 more people from *Titanic's* decks.

Titanic's first lifeboat to be launched was No. 7, at 12.45 a.m. and her last one, Collapsible D, was launched at 2.05 a.m. Therefore her officers managed to launch 18 lifeboats in one hour and twenty minutes. This is an average of one lifeboat every four minutes and twenty-four seconds. This may seem fast, until one realises that during the 25 minutes it took to launch her first 6 lifeboats (No's 7, 5, 3, 8, 1 and 6, respectively) none of her stern 8 were being lowered (No's 9 to 16); and during the 25 minutes it took to launch her stern 8 lifeboats, none of her remaining forward 6 were being lowered. This is because, of *Titanic's* 862 crew, only about 50 were Able Seamen, including Officers, Lookouts and Quartermasters, and only a handful of these were experienced hands who could be really useful in launching lifeboats safely and efficiently. Moreover, six were sent to open *Titanic's* gangway doors and were never seen again; and at least two Able Seamen were sent off in each lifeboat, rapidly depleting those available to launch the remaining boats.

If *Titanic* had had twice as many lifeboats, sufficient to carry all on board, she would have needed twice the number of deck crew, or certainly those she did have would have needed to be very much better trained in launching lifeboats and better organized.

Final Moments

74 CAPTAIN SMITH ADVISED THOSE ON BOARD NEAR THE END TO 'BE BRITISH'.

No. Although this is engraved on his memorial and featured in many films, it's just another myth popularised by the British press at the time. *Titanic*'s passengers were drawn from all over the world and Captain Smith was an experienced transatlantic captain and a cosmopolitan, sophisticated man. Had he been prone to this type of jingoistic statement, he certainly wouldn't have been so popular with the prominent Americans and Canadians who preferred to travel on ships he captained and to dine with him while on board. If he had said 'Be British' to anyone, it would have been to the crew, but not one member of the crew remembers him saying this.

75 THE BAND PLAYED NEARER, MY GOD, TO THEE, AS THE SHIP SANK.

Possibly. The band began by playing light, cheerful music, including waltzes, ragtime tunes, and the popular comic songs of the day from the London music halls, in order to reassure *Titanic*'s passengers after the collision.

Irving Berlin's *Alexander's Ragtime Band* was very popular at the time, and Fourth Officer Boxhall recalled that this was the first tune the band played after the collision, which he noticed as he came through the First Class lounge on the way back from his inspection tour of the ship. Major Arthur Peuchen, Mrs. Lily Futrelle and gambler George Brereton all confirmed that the band played this tune that night.

Another tune that was remembered was *In the Shadows*, which had been a big London hit in 1911. Evidence of the last tune played comes from assistant Marconi operator, Harold Bride, who was quoted as follows in the New York press on 19th April, 1912:

> 'From aft came the tunes of the band. It was a ragtime tune, I don't know what. Then there was *Autumn*. Phillips ran aft, and that was the last I ever saw of him…'

Bride was probably referring to the popular waltz *Songe d'Automne*, composed by Archibald Joyce, which was a major hit in London in 1912.

Fred Vallance, band leader of the Cunard liner Laconia wrote to Walter Lord in 1957, explaining that he was once playing *Songe d'Automne*, and a ship's steward (apparently from the *Titanic*) came up and admonished him that it was 'unlucky'. This tends to add weight to the band playing only cheerful songs, and First Class Titanic survivor Colonel Archibald Gracie observed:

> 'If *Nearer, My God, to Thee* was one of the selections,
> I assuredly would have noticed it and regarded it as a
> tactless warning of immediate death, and more likely
> to create a panic that our special efforts were directed
> towards avoiding…'

In addition, this hymn was set to the tune of *Bethany* in
the US, but J. B. Dykes *Horbury* in the UK (and as band
leader Wallace Hartley had a strong Methodist background,
he would have grown up with it set to Sullivan's *Proprior
Deo*) and these facts suggest that it may therefore have
been unlikely that both American and British passengers
recognised the hymn, as they both claim to have done.

Archibald Grace, in a talk he gave to the Washington
University Club in November 1912, shortly before he died
as a result of exposure he suffered the night the *Titanic* sank,
said that the band stopped playing about half an hour before
the ship sank and added that he himself saw the musicians
lay down their instruments. This was confirmed by another
First Class passenger, A. H. Barkworth, who said:

> 'I do not wish to detract from the bravery of anybody,
> but I might mention that when I first came on deck
> the band was playing a waltz. The next time I passed
> where the band had been stationed, the members had
> thrown down their instruments, and were not to be
> seen.'

However, it is possible that the band only laid down their
instruments while they went to their quarters to get their

lifebelts. Survivor Pierre Marechal told Secretary Williams of the Amalgamated Musicians' Union that the musicians were not wearing lifebelts and secretary Williams later wrote:

> 'Marechal declared that the musicians received an order to play all the time without stopping, so as to avoid a panic. They were placed on the deck, that is to say, between the decks [on A deck]. Marechal specially noticed that none of them had lifebelts, he being convinced that in giving them these orders their lives were to be sacrificed to avoid disorder on board.'

Pierre Marechal took a seat in the very first lifeboat to leave the *Titanic*, but by the time *Titanic* survivor Mrs Gold—who left in a later lifeboat—observed the band, they clearly were wearing lifebelts:

> 'When we left the ship men were sitting on A deck, smoking cigarettes and tapping time with their feet to the music of the band. These passengers and the bandsmen, too, had their lifebelts beside them, and I was specially struck by a glimpse of a violinist playing steadily with a great lifebelt in front of him. The music was ragtime just then.'

It seems quite possible, then, that *Titanic*'s musicians returned to A deck with their lifebelts and then continued playing their music where they had left off. In which case the possibility also remains that, in the final half-hour before the vessel sank, the bandsmen may have chosen to forego their repertoire of lively music and concentrate instead on playing inspiring selections, including hymns, in order to instil courage in those who remained on the *Titanic* after all the lifeboats had departed.

Indeed, Mrs. Paul Schabert said that, after playing ragtime for a while, the band began playing hymns, and that *When we Meet Beyond* was one of the first hymns they chose, followed by others; Dr. Washington Dodge, from his lifeboat, reported hearing the band playing *Lead, Kindly Light*; a group of Titanic crewmen heard the band play *Abide With Me* and *Eternal Father, Strong To Save* as well as other hymns. Marie Jerwan mentions that the band played *Nearer, My God, To Thee* in the following extract from a letter she wrote in May of 1912:

> 'Little by little the lights disappeared one after another, until we could see only a black mass. The bow was already submerged. We still heard the musicians of the ship playing the beautiful hymn: *Nearer My God to Thee*, to which we joined in with all our heart. What heroism to stay that way at their post to give courage to those who were going to die, in playing this song, so beautiful and so solemn.'

And finally, we have wireless operator Harold Bride's account of *Autumn*, which could also have been the hymn tune *Autumn*. Although newspaper reports and survivor accounts can be inaccurate, Rev. Burke and Rev. McCarthy, both *Carpathia* passengers, were told about the hymn *Nearer, My God, To Thee* by survivors while the rescue ship was still at sea;

and both Kate Buss and Edwina Troutt mentioned having heard that hymn played when they wrote to friends whilst still on board the *Carpathia*. Steward Edward Wheelton agreed with Miss Troutt, telling a reporter that, before the final plunge, the bandsmen changed the cheerful character of their musical program and played the hymn *Nearer, My God, To Thee*.

Another steward, Jacob Gibbons, was adamant that this was indeed the case; according to Gibbons:

> 'The cries of those on board were terrible, and I doubt whether the memory of them will ever leave me during my lifetime. It has been denied by many that the band was playing, but it was doing so and the strains of *Nearer, My God, to Thee* came clearly over the water with a solemnity so awful that words cannot express it.'

Moreover, the objection that this hymn would have been unrecognisable to both American and British passengers, due to its different settings on each side of the Atlantic is dealt with when one recalls that *Nearer, My God, To Thee* was in fact on bandmaster Wallace Hartley's White Star Line play list. It would therefore have been played during religious services on board and both British and American passengers would by 15th April have associated the same tune with *Nearer, My God, To Thee*.

Indeed, Elwane Moody, a well-known Leeds musician, was a close friend of Wallace Hartley and had just completed twenty-two Atlantic crossings with him on the *Mauretania*.

(In fact, Hartley had asked Moody to accompany him on the *Titanic*, but Moody had declined.) Not long before the *Titanic*'s maiden voyage, Moody asked Hartley, 'What would you do if you were ever on a ship that was sinking?' Hartley looked thoughtful for a moment and replied: 'I don't think I could do better than play *O God, Our Help In Ages Past* or *Nearer, My God, To Thee.*' Later, after the disaster, Moody said, 'When I read the statement in the papers that he had gone to his death leading the band in *Nearer, My God, To Thee*, I believed it. If it had been some other hymn I might not have done so, but as it is I can quite believe it. It is just what he would do.'

And Lewis Cross, double bass player on the *Celtic*, was another friend of Wallace Hartley who once spoke with him about the possibility of a shipwreck. Hartley smiled and said, 'Well, I don't suppose it will ever happen, but you know music is a bigger weapon than a gun in a big emergency, and I think that a band could do more to calm passengers than all the officers.'

We do not know if *Nearer, My God, To Thee* was the final hymn played by the *Titanic*'s band, but there is plenty of survivor evidence that hymns—and this hymn in particular—were played that night.

Regardless of what was actually the final tune played that night, and whether it was ragtime or hymns, the music of *Titanic*'s band evidently made a deep impression on many survivors, both during the disaster and afterwards. The Countess of Rothes, who was rescued in lifeboat No. 8, told Walter Lord how, when dining out with friends about a year after the sinking, she suddenly 'experienced the feeling of cold and intense horror she always associated with the *Titanic*. A moment later, she realised that it was because the orchestra was playing selections from the *Tales of Hoffman*, which had been played by the *Titanic's* band after dinner on Sunday evening, 14th April, 1912.

76 TITANIC'S MARCONI OPERATORS KNOCKED A STOKER UNCONSCIOUS AND LEFT HIM TO DIE.

Yes. Bride and Phillips did overcome a stoker who was attempting to steal Phillips' lifejacket. Bride referred to this incident in his testimony at the British inquiry:

> 16774: 'Have you made a statement at any time that you found Mr. Phillips being attacked or his lifebelt being removed?'
> 'Someone was taking the lifebelt off Phillips when I left the cabin.'
> 16775: 'Do I understand you to state that you thought it was a stoker who was taking this lifebelt off Mr. Phillips?'
> 'I presumed from the appearance of the man that he was someone in that line of business.'
> 16776: 'This would have been a few minutes before you left the room?'
> 'Yes.'
> 16777: 'Was he dressed in stoker's gear?'
> 'Yes.'

16778: 'Do I understand that you hit him, or what?'

'Well, we stopped him from taking the lifebelt off.'

16779: '"We," you say?'

'Yes.'

16780: 'I understood the report was that Mr. Phillips was engaged at this time with his work?'

'Yes.'

16781: 'Sending messages; and that you forced this man away?'

'Well, I forced the man away and it attracted Mr. Phillips's attention, and he came and assisted me.'

16782: 'Is your recollection of this matter very clear?'

'It is fairly clear.'

16783: 'Would you know the man again if you saw him?'

'I am not likely to see him.'

16784: 'You are supposed to have hit him?'

'Well, I held him and Mr. Phillips hit him.'

16785: 'Mr. Phillips hit him?'

'Yes.'

16786: 'That is the difference between what you say and what I read. You are absolutely positive on this question?'

'I am positive on it, yes.'

Nothing more is known of what happened to the man, although if he was only knocked unconscious it is possible he would have been brought round by the seawater as it reached the wireless room. Bride and Phillips didn't leave this room until about 10 minutes before the *Titanic* sank, so it's not surprising there's no mention of what happened to the man after he was overpowered by them. The incident was not pursued further at the inquiry after it was ascertained that it was Phillips, who did not survive, rather than Bride, who actually hit the man.

77 ISMAY PUSHED HIS WAY INTO COLLAPSIBLE C, THE LAST LIFEBOAT TO BE LAUNCHED ON THE STARBOARD SIDE.

Probably not. Ismay got into the last lifeboat to be lowered on the starboard side, Collapsible C, at about 2 a.m., only when it was actually in the act of being lowered away and when there were no passengers in sight, as he explained at the US Inquiry:

JBI547: (Senator Smith) 'Was it filled to its capacity?'
'No; it was not.
JBI548: Why?'
'I understand the full capacity of one of those boats is about 60 to 65.'
JBI549: 'Of the collapsible?'
'I do not know whether the capacity of the collapsible is the same as that of the wooden boat.'
JBI550: 'It was not filled to its capacity?'
'No, sir.'
JBI551: 'Do you know how many people were in it?'

'I should think there were about 40 women in it, and some children. There was a child in arms. I think they were all third class passengers, so far as I could see.'

JBI552: 'And this boat was from the starboard side of the boat deck, or top deck, near the bridge?'

'Yes, sir.'

JBI553: 'At the time you entered it, did you say anything to the captain about entering it?'

'No, sir; I did not. I never saw the captain.'

JBI554: 'Did he say anything to you about your entering it?'

'No, sir.'

JBI555: 'Who, if any one, told you to enter that lifeboat?'

'No one, sir.'

JBI556: 'Why did you enter it?'

'Because there was room in the boat. She was being lowered away. I felt the ship was going down, and I got into the boat.'

Lord Mersey accepted Ismay's version of events, concluding in his Report at the end of the British Inquiry:

'As to the attack on Mr. Bruce Ismay, it resolved itself into the suggestion that, occupying the position of Managing Director of the Steamship Company, some moral duty was imposed upon him to wait on board until the vessel foundered. I do not agree. Mr. Ismay, after rendering assistance to many passengers, found

'C' collapsible, the last boat on the starboard side, actually being lowered. No other people were there at the time. There was room for him and he jumped in. (Ismay, 18559) Had he not jumped in he would merely have added one more life, namely, his own, to the number of those lost.'

It should be noted that, prior to his departure in Collapsible C, Ismay had worked tirelessly all night alongside *Titanic*'s crew to get the lifeboats away as quickly as possible. Third Officer Pitman testified:

'I came along and brought in my boat. I stood on it and said, "Come along, ladies." There was a big crowd. Mr. Ismay helped to get them along; assisted in every way. We got the boat nearly full, and I shouted out for any more ladies.'

Ismay personally helped and urged scores of women to get into lifeboats, many of whom might not otherwise have done so; at one point he practically threw First Class passenger Edith Russell down the stairs from the boat deck in his haste to get her into lifeboat No. 11, which was being loaded from the A Deck rail. Two First Class stewardesses, Annie Martin and Katherine Gold, remembered him urging women into a lifeboat in an interview with the *Western Daily Mercury*, 30 April 1912:

'Mr. Bruce Ismay helped all he could to get the women into the boats. He implored one group of stewardesses to take their place with the others. The reply was: "But we are only stewardesses, sir!" when he said: "You are women; please get in at once," and he insisted on their doing so. "We saw him later on when he was sitting on the gunwale of one of the last boats to leave. He had nothing on but his pyjamas and an overcoat and was blue with the cold."'

In fact, Ismay was so anxious about getting the boats loaded that at one point a somewhat exasperated Fifth Officer Lowe ordered him away from lifeboat No. 5, in language described at the inquiry as 'not very parliamentary':

HGL332: 'Do you know any of the men who assisted you in lowering that lifeboat?'

'No, sir; I do not, by name. But there is a man here, and had he not been here I should not have known that I had ordered Mr. Ismay away from the boat.'

HGL333: 'Did you order Mr. Ismay away from the boat?'

'I did, sir.'

HGL334: 'What did you say to him?'

'This was on the starboard side. I don't know his name, but I know him by sight. He is a steward. He spoke to me on board the *Carpathia*. He asked me if I knew what I had said to Mr. Ismay. I said, "I don't know Mr. Ismay. "Well," he said, "you used very, very strong language with him." I said, "Did I?" I said, "I can not help it if I did." He said, "Yes, you did," and he repeated the words. If you wish me to repeat them

I will do so; if you do not, I will not.'

HGL335: 'I will first ask you this: What was the occasion for your using this harsh language to Mr. Ismay?'

'The occasion for using the language I did was because Mr. Ismay was overanxious and he was getting a trifle excited. He said, "Lower away! Lower away! Lower away! Lower away!" I said—well, let it be—'

Mr. Ismay: 'Give us what you said.'

Mr. Lowe: 'The chairman is examining me.'

Senator Smith: 'Mr. Ismay, you asked the witness to give the language?

Mr. Ismay: 'I have no objection to his giving it. It was not very parliamentary.'

Senator Smith: 'If the language is inappropriate—'

Mr. Lowe: 'There is only one word that might be so considered.'

Mr. Ismay: 'May I suggest that it be put on a piece of paper and given to you, Mr. Chairman, and you decide.'

Senator Smith: 'All right; write it down.

(The witness, Mr. Lowe, wrote something on a piece of paper and handed it to the chairman.) HGL336: 'You may put that into the record. You said you—'

'You wish me to repeat it, sir?'

HGL337: 'You uttered this to Mr. Ismay?'

'Yes; that was in the heat of the moment.'

HGL338: 'What was the occasion of it; because of his excitement, because of his anxiety?'

'Because he was, in a way, interfering with my duties,

and also, of course, he only did this because he was anxious to get the people away and also to help me.'

HGL339: 'What did you say to him?'

'Do you want me to repeat that statement?'

HGL340: 'Yes, sir.'

'I told him, "If you will get to hell out of that I shall be able to do something."'

HGL341: 'What reply did he make?'

'He did not make any reply. I said, "Do you want me to lower away quickly?" I said, "You will have me drown the whole lot of them." I was on the floor myself lowering away.'

HGL342: 'You were on the boat deck, standing on the deck of the boat, the upper deck; and where did he stand?'

'He was at the ship's side, like this (indicating). This is the ship—he was hanging on the davit like this (indicating). He said, "Lower away, lower away, lower away," and I was slacking away just here at his feet (indicating).'

HGL343: 'The boat was being lowered?'

'I was lowering away the boat myself, personally.'

HGL344: 'I want you to say what he did after you said this to him?'

'He walked away; and then he went to No. 3 boat.'

HGL345: 'Alongside of yours?'

'The next boat forward of mine; that is, on the same side; and I think he went ahead there on his own hook, getting things ready there, to the best of his ability.'

Lowe also observed Ismay at no.3:

> HGL505: 'Did Mr. Ismay assist in filling that boat?'
> 'Yes; he assisted there, too.'
> HGL506: 'You found him there when you turned from No. 5 to No. 3?'
> 'He was there, and I distinctly remember seeing him alongside of me—that is, by my side—when the first detonator went off. I will tell you how I happen to remember it so distinctly. It was because the flash of the detonator lit up the whole deck, I did not know who Mr. Ismay was then, but I learned afterwards who he was, and he was standing alongside of me.'
> HGL507: 'Did you say anything to him?'
> 'I did not.'
> HGL508: 'You saw him in the flash—'
> 'Of the detonator.'

This impression of Ismay working like the crew to get lifeboat No. 3 away is reinforced by the testimony of Samuel Rule:

> 6462: 'At this time, from what you have said, Mr. Ismay was standing close?'
> 'Yes, he was helping to get No. 3 out.'
> 6463: 'Helping to get No. 3 boat out?'
> 'Yes.'
> 6464: (The Attorney-General—To the Witness.) 'Was Mr. Ismay dressed at this time?'
> 'No, he had his slippers and a light overcoat on and no hat.'

6465: 'Slippers, light overcoat and no hat?'
'Yes.'
6466: 'You said he was helping. What was he doing?'
'He was just the same as any of the crew; he was doing all he could to assist to get the boats out.'

The evidence that Ismay pushed himself into a lifeboat comes from the following privately published account of First Class passenger Jack Thayer, written in 1940, three years after Ismay's death:

'There was some disturbance in loading the last two forward starboard boats. A large crowd of men was pressing to get into them. No women were around as far as I could see. I saw Ismay, who had been assisting in the loading of the last boat, push his way into it. It was really every man for himself…'

This account seems to ring true, but it was written long after the disaster and Jack Thayer had every reason to be critical of Ismay, not least because his father was killed in the disaster.

Billy Carter, the other First Class passenger who escaped in this lifeboat with Ismay, insisted in 1912 that Ismay's version of events was accurate. Although Mr Carter may have had similar reasons for agreeing that Ismay's escape was as Ismay testified, his account was given at the time and must therefore be given the weight it deserves, regardless of what one thinks of Carter's own character. (Carter's wife divorced him soon after the disaster, citing cruelty as one of her reasons.)

Given that Ismay was clearly working alongside *Titanic*'s

crew, and as crew, it is most likely that he simply stepped in, as he said he did, as the boat was in the act of being lowered, as he would have had the opportunity of doing so.

Regardless of which version of events was most accurate, public opinion in 1912 damned Ismay for saving himself from the loss of what was effectively his own ship, when so many men and women drowned, especially given that it was known that he was desirous of making a fast passage. The press at the time dubbed him 'J. BRUTE Ismay.'

It seems that Ismay's own conscience was not clear on the matter of his survival. On board the rescue ship *Carpathia*, Ismay could not face any of the 37 women whose husbands had drowned on the *Titanic*. He therefore hid in the doctor's cabin for the entire passage to New York, though he explained this differently to Senator Smith at the US Inquiry, at 10.30 a.m. on the morning after the *Carpathia* arrived in New York:

> JBI560: 'Not desiring to be impertinent at all, but in order that I may not be charged with omitting to do my duty, I would like to know where you went after you boarded the *Carpathia*, and how you happened to go there?'
>
> 'Mr. Chairman, I understand that my behaviour on board the *Titanic*, and subsequently on board the *Carpathia*, has been very severely criticized. I want to court the fullest inquiry, and I place myself unreservedly in the hands of yourself and any of your colleagues, to ask me any questions in regard to my conduct; so please do not hesitate to do so, and I will

answer them to the best of my ability. So far as the *Carpathia* is concerned, sir, when I got on board the ship I stood up with my back against the bulkhead, and somebody came up to me and said, "Will you not go into the saloon and get some soup, or something to drink?" "No," I said, "I really do not want anything at all." He said, "Do go and get something." I said, "No. If you will leave me alone I will be very much happier here." I said, "If you will get me in some room where I can be quiet, I wish you would." He said, "Please go in the saloon and get something hot." I said, "I would rather not." Then he took me and put me into a room. I did not know whose the room was, at all. This man proved to be the doctor of the *Carpathia*. I was in that room until I left the ship. I was never outside the door of that room. During the whole of the time I was in this room, I never had anything of a solid nature, at all; I lived on soup. I did not want very much of anything.'

78 TITANIC'S ENGINEERS DIED AT THEIR POSTS BELOW DECKS.

No. Whilst the engineers were undoubtedly all very brave, and stayed at their posts until they were discharged, they did not in fact die at their posts. When it became obvious that nothing more could be done, and the flooding was too severe for the pumps to cope, they all came up onto *Titanic's* open well deck, but by this time all the lifeboats had already left.

Greaser Frederick Scott remembered seeing all the engineers on deck at the end:

5685: (Sir Rufus) 'When you were looking over the starboard side was there anybody near you?'

'Yes, all the engineers and firemen and all that.'

5686: 'All the engineers?'

'Yes.'

5687: 'Do you mean the Officers?'

'Yes; the engineers that were on watch.'

5688: 'Then, if I understand it aright, all the engineers had come up too?'

'They were all at the top.'

5689: 'Did they come up when you came up?'

'Just afterwards, but some of them went up on the boat deck with me. They came up the [escape] ladder just behind me.'

5690: 'When you say they were standing there, where were they standing?'

'Just against the electric crane aft.'

5691: 'Will you indicate to us on the model where that is?'

'Yes, just about here.' (Pointing on the model.)

5692: 'On the boat deck?'

'On the boat deck.'

5693: 'That is the last you saw of them?'

'That is the last I saw of them.'

79 TITANIC'S BOILERS EXPLODED AS SHE SANK.

No. This was a misconception brought about by witnesses such as Able Seaman Frank Osman, who said that he heard, and saw, an explosion as the ship sank which he thought was caused by cold seawater cracking the hot boilers. Osman remembers that the smoke came up through the funnels along with pieces of coal, which made him think that the boilers had exploded. However, Robert Ballard, who discovered the wreck lying in two sections on the seabed, found the boilers more or less intact, making it impossible that they had exploded. The noise of an 'explosion' which Osman and others heard was actually the noise of *Titanic* breaking up and everything on her breaking loose and crashing through the ship, as she tipped up before her final plunge.

Boilers are unlikely to explode on contact with cold seawater, although many believed this was the case. A far more likely cause of boiler explosions is a build-up of steam, but this was prevented by the safety valves on the boilers and by the quick action of the firemen, who managed to draw the fires from all the lit boilers, although they were soon up to their knees in water. *Titanic's* engines appear to have run for a few minutes following the collision, according to greaser Frederick Scott, but after she stopped the safety valves lifted, letting a great deal of steam off as the lifeboats were being loaded and producing the loud noise which made communication on the boat deck almost impossible.

Archibald Gracie put the same 'explosion' noise down to machinery and furniture falling through the ship and smashing through the transverse watertight bulkheads as they went. Lawrence Beesley, in his book *The Loss of the Titanic*, also attributed the noise to machinery falling through the ship, describing the noise as a sustained kind of crash:

> '...[T]here came a noise which many people, wrongly I think, have described as an explosion... It was partly a groan, partly a rattle, and partly a smash, and it was not a sudden roar as an explosion would be; it went on successively for some seconds, possibly fifteen to twenty... It was as if all the heavy things one could think of had been thrown downstairs from the top of a house, smashing each other and the stairs and everything in the way.'

80 TITANIC BROKE IN HALF AS SHE SANK.

Yes. This fact was not generally believed until 1985, when Robert Ballard found *Titanic*'s wreck on the seabed, nearly 4,500 metres below the surface. Her bow section was lying more than 650 metres north of her stern section. Until this discovery it was generally accepted that *Titanic* had sunk in one piece, despite a number of witnesses who said that they saw her break in half.

James Cameron's 1997 film *Titanic* shows the stern section rising to about 45 degrees and then the ship splitting in two from the top down, with her boat deck ripping apart. However, recent forensic studies of the wreck have all concluded that *Titanic*'s hull began to break at a much shallower angle of about 15 degrees. This is not surprising, because the bending moment acting upon the hull would have been much stronger at this shallow angle. As *Titanic* expert Sam Halpern points out, just try holding a baseball bat out at arm's length, and you will see it feels 'lighter' if you begin to point it upwards. *Titanic*'s hull girder was simply not designed to support the stern at a 15 degree angle and therefore it began to break up.

The initial failure of *Titanic*'s hull may have been what Chief Baker Charles Joughin heard when he was getting a drink of water from the A deck pantry:

6040: 'I went to the deck pantry, and while I was in there I thought I would take a drink of water, and while I was getting the drink of water I heard a kind of a crash as if something had buckled, as if part of the ship had buckled, and then I heard a rush overhead.'
6041: 'Do you mean a rush of people?'
'Yes, a rush of people overhead on the deck.'
6042: 'Is the deck pantry on A deck?'
'Yes.'
6043: 'So that the deck above would be the boat deck?'
'Yes, I could hear it.'
6044: 'You could hear it?'
'Yes.'
6045: 'People running—yes?'
6049: 'You say that you heard this sound of buckling or crackling. Was it loud; could anybody in the ship hear it?'

'You could have heard it, but you did not really know what it was. It was not an explosion or anything like that. It was like as if the iron was parting.'
6050: 'Like the breaking of metal?'
'Yes.'

As the break-up continued, 17-year-old First Class passenger Jack Thayer described the sound of it from the forward part of *Titanic's* boat deck:

'Occasionally there had been a muffled thud or deadened explosion within the ship. Now, without warning she seemed to start forward, moving forward and into the water at an angle of about fifteen degrees. This movement with the water rushing up toward us was accompanied by a rumbling roar, mixed with more muffled explosions. It was like standing under a steel railway bridge while an express train passes overhead mingled with the noise of a pressed steel factory and wholesale breakage of china.'

Thayer was then thrown into the water and watched the rest of *Titanic's* break-up from only 40 yards away:

'The cold was terrific. The shock of the water took the breath out of my lungs. Down and down I went, spinning in all directions. Swimming as hard as I could in the direction which I thought to be away from the ship, I finally came up with my lungs bursting, but not having taken any water. The ship was in front of me, forty yards away... The water was over the base of the first funnel. The ship seemed to be surrounded with a glare, and stood out of the night as though she were on fire... The water was over the base of the first funnel. The mass of people on board were surging back, always back toward the floating stern. The rumble and roar continued, with even louder distinct wrenchings and tearings of boilers and engines from their beds. Suddenly the whole superstructure of the ship appeared to split, well forward to midship, and bow or buckle upwards.'

As *Titanic*'s hull split apart, her stern settled back onto an even keel. Many survivors noticed the stern righting itself and some assumed that it would then stay afloat.

Greaser Thomas Dillon observed her fourth funnel falling as *Titanic*'s stern settled back on the water:

3857: (The Commissioner) 'Am I to understand that you were actually on board the *Titanic* when she went down?'
   'Yes, my Lord.'
3858: (Mr. Raymond Asquith) 'Before the ship actually went down did you see her make any movements?'
   'Yes, she took one final plunge and righted herself again.'
3859: 'She gave a plunge and righted herself again?'
   'Yes.'
3860: 'Did you notice anything about the funnel?'
   'Not then.'

3861: 'Did you afterwards notice something about the funnel?'

'Yes.'

3862: 'What?'

'When she went down.'

3863: 'Was that after you had left the ship?'

'Before I left the ship.'

3864: 'What did you notice?'

'Well, the funnel seemed to cant up towards me.'

3865: 'It seemed to fall aft?'

'Yes; it seemed to fall up this way.'

3866: 'Was that the aftermost funnel?'

'Yes.'

3867: 'Did you get the idea that the ship was breaking in two?'

'No.'

3868: 'Did the funnel seem to fall towards you?'

'Yes.'

3869: (The Commissioner) 'That is the after funnel?'

'Yes, my Lord.'

3870: (Mr. Raymond Asquith) 'Then you say the ship plunged and righted herself again; and was it then that you dived into the water?'

'I did not dive into the water.'

3871: 'How did you get off the ship into the water?'

'I went down with the ship, and shoved myself away from her into the water.'

3872: 'Were you sucked down at all?'

'About two fathoms [12 feet].'

In fact, although *Titanic*'s stern had momentarily settled back on an even keel as her hull split, her bow and stern sections had not completely separated. As *Titanic*'s flooded bow section made for the bottom, it dragged the forward end of the buoyant stern section down with it, upending it again. Evidently the remaining attachments were not symmetrical and *Titanic*'s stern twisted around as it sank.

Jack Thayer continued to observe this at close hand, from his vantage point in the water, but only after he had been washed 10 or 20 yards further away by the falling of *Titanic*'s first funnel, and then clambered aboard the bottom of upturned Collapsible B:

'I pulled myself up as far as I could almost exhausted, but could not get my legs up. I asked them to give me a hand up, which they readily did. Sitting on my haunches and holding on for dear life, I was again facing the *Titanic*. There was the gigantic mass, about fifty or sixty yards away. The forward motion had stopped. She was pivoting on a point just abaft of midship. Her stern was gradually rising into the air, seemingly in no hurry, just slowly and deliberately. Her deck was turned slightly toward us. We could see groups of the almost fifteen hundred people aboard, clinging in clusters or bunches, like swarming bees; only to fall in masses, pairs or singly, as the great part of the ship, two hundred and fifty feet of it, rose into the sky, till it reached a sixty-five or seventy degree angle. Here it seemed to pause, and just hung, for what felt like minutes. Gradually she turned her deck away from us, as though to hide from our sight the awful spectacle.

'I looked upwards—we were right under the three enormous propellers. For an instant, I thought they were sure to come down on top of us. Then, with the deadened noise of the bursting of her last few gallant bulkheads, she slid quietly away from us into the sea.'

Chief Baker Charles Joughin was one of those who remained on the ship during this final plunge and he graphically recalls the awful scene:

6052: 'What did you do?'

'I kept out of the crush as much as I possibly could, and I followed down—followed down getting towards the well of the deck, and just as I got down towards the well she gave a great list over to port and threw everybody in a bunch except myself. I did not see anybody else besides myself out of the bunch.'

6053: 'That was when you were in the well, was it?'

'I was not exactly in the well, I was on the side, practically on the side then. She threw them over. At last I clambered on the side when she chucked them.'

6054: 'You mean the starboard side?'

'The starboard side.'

6055: 'The starboard was going up and she took a lurch to port?'

'It was not going up, but the other side was going down.'

6056: 'It is very difficult to say how many, I daresay,

but could you give me some idea, of how many people there were in this crush?'

'I have no idea, Sir; I know they were piled up.'

6057: 'What do you mean when you say, "No idea." Were there hundreds?'

'Yes, there were more than that—many hundreds, I should say.'

6058: (The Solicitor-General) 'You said this vessel took a lurch to port and threw them in a heap. Did she come back; did she right herself at all?'

'No, Sir.'

6059: 'She took a lurch and she did not return?'

'She did not return.'

6060: 'Can you tell us what happened to you?'

'Yes, I eventually got on to the starboard side of the poop.'

6064: 'On the side of the ship?'

'Yes.'

6070: 'Did you find anybody else holding that rail there, on the poop?'

'No.'

6071: 'You were the only one?'

'I did not see anybody else.'

6072: 'Were you holding the rail so that you were inside the ship, or were you holding the rail so that you were on the outside of the ship?'

'On the outside.'

6073: 'So that the rail was between you and the deck?'

'Yes.'

6074: 'Then what happened?'

'Well, I was just wondering what next to do. I had tightened my belt and I had transferred some things out of this pocket into my stern pocket. I was just wondering what next to do when she went.'

6075: 'And did you find yourself in the water?'

'Yes.'

6076: 'Did you feel that you were dragged under or did you keep on the top of the water?'

'I do not believe my head went under the water at all. It may have been wetted, but no more.'

Titanic's entire sinking sequence is neatly summarised by Lookout George Symons who was watching from lifeboat No. 1 between 200 and 500 yards away. Symons was regarded by Lightoller as possessing remarkable eyesight and as the best lookout, this is what he told the British Inquiry:

11502: 'Now, just one moment. Just tell us why you say "after I saw the ship was doomed" you pulled away 200 yards? What was it that you saw that made you think that?'

'Because her forecastle head was well under water then. Her lights had all disappeared then. You could see her starboard sidelight, which was still burning, was not so very far from the water, and her stern was well up in the air.'

11503: 'When you say all her lights went out, do you mean right away astern too?'

'No, just her foremost lights had disappeared, and

her starboard sidelight left burning was the only light, barring the masthead light, on that side of the bridge that I could see.'

11504: 'Then you saw her with her stern out?'

'Yes.'

11505: 'Will you give us an idea what angle was her stern as far as you could see? How did it look to you; was it all up?'

'More like that with a cant. (Describing.) I do not know what position you would call it altogether.'

11506: 'Was it out of water?'

'Yes.'

11507: 'Did you see her keel?'

'No, you could not see her keel.'

11508: (The Commissioner) 'Could you see the propellers?'

'You could just see the propellers.'

11509: (The Attorney-General) 'You could see the propellers?'

'Yes.'

11510: 'Then when you saw her like that, what was the next thing that happened?'

'A little while after that we pulled a little way and lay on the oars again. The other boats were around us by that time, and some were pulling further away from us. I stood and watched it till I heard two sharp explosions in the ship. What they were I could not say. Then she suddenly took a top cant, her stern came well out of the water then.'

11511: 'A top cant?'

'You know what I mean to say, she took a heavy cant and her bow went down clear.'

11512: 'Head downwards?'

'Head down, and that is the time when I saw her lights go out, all her lights. The next thing I saw was her poop. As she went down like that so her poop righted itself and I thought to myself, "The poop is going to float." It could not have been more than two or three minutes after that that her poop went up as straight as anything; there was a sound like steady thunder as you hear on an ordinary night at a distance, and soon she disappeared from view.'

11517: 'I understand you to say that at one period you saw her stern right itself?'

'It righted itself without the bow; in my estimation she must have broken in half.'

11518: 'Can you form any idea from what part of the vessel it was that she appeared to right herself?'

'I should think myself it was abaft the after expansion plate.'

11521: 'Where was it?'

'I should say it would be about abeam of the after funnel, or a little forward.'

11523: (The Attorney-General.) 'Then you saw her right herself—this part of her?'

'Yes; I saw the poop right itself.'

11524: 'And then it went up?'

'Yes; then it went up and disappeared from view.'

11525: 'And then went right down?'

'Yes.'

Unfortunately, although *Titanic's* most senior surviving officer, Charles Herbert Lightoller, saw the ship's stern rising high out of the water during the final phase of her sinking, he did not observe her breaking in two, as this happened while he was being sucked underwater by the sinking *Titanic*, before he was blown free by a blast of hot air and reached collapsible B. Lightoller therefore erroneously assumed from the stern's upright attitude that the part of *Titanic* he couldn't see was intact, and believed she had sunk in one piece:

> 14074: (The Solicitor-General) 'I do not know whether you can help us at all in describing what happened to the ship. You were engaged and had other things to think about; but what did happen to the ship? Can you tell us at all?'
>
> (Lightoller) 'Are you referring to the reports of the ship breaking in two?'
> 14075: 'Yes?'
> 'It is utterly untrue. The ship did not and could not have broken in two.'
> 14092: (The Solicitor-General) 'Did you continue watching the afterpart sufficiently to be able to tell us whether the afterpart settled on the water at all?'
> 'It did not settle on the water.'
> 14093: 'You are confident it did not?'
> 'Perfectly certain.'
> The Solicitor-General: 'Your Lordship knows a lot of Witnesses have said their impression was the afterpart settled on the water.'
> 14094: (The Commissioner) 'I have heard that over

and over again.' (To the witness.) 'That you say is not true?'

'That is not true, My Lord. I was watching her keenly the whole time.'

14097: 'Just tell us what happened, as you saw it?'

'After she reached an angle of 50 or 60 degrees, or something about that, there was this rumbling sound, which I attributed to the boilers leaving their beds and crushing down on or through the bulkheads. The ship at that time was becoming more perpendicular, until finally she attained the absolute perpendicular— somewhere about that position (Describing), and then went slowly down. She went down very slowly until the end, and then, after she got so far (Describing), the afterpart of the second cabin deck, she, of course, went down much quicker.'

Both the American and British Inquiries accepted Lightoller's incomplete version of events, which were regarded as accurate for 73 years, until Ballard found the *Titanic*.

81 COL. JOHN JACOB ASTOR IV WAS CRUSHED BY A FALLING FUNNEL AS THE SHIP SANK.

No. This has generally been accepted as fact, probably because of the following statement by First Class survivor, Colonel Archibald Gracie:

'From the fact that I never saw Colonel Astor on the Boat Deck later, and also because his body, when found, was crushed (according to the statement of one who saw it at Halifax, Mr. Harry K. White, of Boston, Mr. Edward A. Kent's brother-in-law, my schoolmate and friend from boyhood), I am of the opinion that he met his fate on the ship when the boilers tore through it, as described later.'

However, Gerald Ross, an electrician on the *Mackay-Bennett*, the ship which recovered the bodies of most of the *Titanic*'s victims, informed the *Philadelphia Evening Bulletin*:

'I saw the recovery of Col. Astor's body. Like the others it was floating buoyed by a lifebelt. Both arms extended upwards. The face was swollen, one jaw was injured. His body was clothed in a business suit and tan shoes. His watch, a costly thing, studded with diamonds, was dangling from his pocket. It had stopped at 3:20. Practically all the other watches on bodies we recovered had stopped at 2:10. His watch chain was of platinum and so were the settings of the rings he wore.'

Astor's jaw injury was relatively slight and could have been caused by his lifebelt, if he jumped from *Titanic*, or by other drowning passengers or debris as the ship sank. The *Mackay-Bennett*'s description of body no. 124, which was identified as Astor from the effects found with it, made no mention of either serious injury or blackening:

NO. 124—MALE—ESTIMATED AGE 50—LIGHT HAIR & MOUSTACHE

CLOTHING—Blue serge suit; blue handkerchief with 'A.V.'; belt with gold buckle; brown boots with red rubber soles; brown flannel shirt; 'J.J.A.' on back of collar.

EFFECTS—Gold watch; cuff links, gold with diamond; diamond ring with three stones; £225 in English notes; $2440 in notes; £5 in gold; 7s. in silver; 5 ten franc pieces; gold pencil; pocketbook.

FIRST CLASS NAME—J.J.ASTOR

John Snow, an undertaker aboard the ship, said that the body was in an 'excellent state of preservation', and Captain Roberts, the commander of Astor's yacht, saw his body at Halifax and said his features were unharmed and only slightly discoloured by water.

82 FIRST OFFICER MURDOCH SHOT ONE OR TWO PASSENGERS BEFORE SHOOTING HIMSELF.

Yes, this is probably true. At about 1 a.m., all *Titanic*'s officers had been issued with Webley revolvers, as Lightoller recalled in his memoirs *Titanic and Other Ships*:

'It was about this time [the launching of lifeboat No. 6] that the Chief Officer came over from the starboard side and asked, did I know where the firearms were? I told the Chief Officer, "Yes, I know where they are. Come along and I'll get them for you," and into the First Officer's cabin we went——the Chief, Murdoch, the Captain and myself——where I hauled them out, still in all their pristine newness and grease. I was going out when the Chief shoved one of the revolvers into my hands, with a handful of ammunition, and said, "Here you are, you may need it."'

Later, as he was struggling in the water, Lightoller noticed the weight of his revolver was dragging him down:

'For a time I wondered what was making it so difficult for me to keep my head above the water. Time and again I went under, until it dawned on me that it was the great Webley revolver, still in my pocket, that was dragging me down. I soon sent that on its downward journey.'

Fifth Officer Lowe was the first to use his gun that night, at about 1.15 a.m., firing several warning shots between lifeboat No. 14 and the side of the ship, in order to stop a group of men from rushing it. Greaser Frederick Scott saw this incident:

5657: 'And one of the boats was where the Officer

pulled a revolver out and shot it between the ship and the boat and said, "If any man jumps into the boat I will shoot him like a dog."'

Lightoller also threatened passengers with his gun at about 1.45 a.m., when a group of men tried to get into emergency lifeboat number 2, as he recalled in his memoirs, *Titanic And Other Ships*, though he said it was not loaded at the time:

> 'Arriving alongside the emergency boat, someone spoke out of the darkness, and said "There are men in that boat." I jumped in, and discovered that there actually were... They hopped out mighty quickly, and I encouraged them verbally, also by vigorously flourishing my revolver. They certainly thought they were between the devil and the deep blue sea in more senses than one, and I had the satisfaction of seeing them tumbling head over heels, preferring the uncertain safety of the deck, to the cold lead, which I suppose they fully imagined would follow their disobedience—so much for imagination—the revolver was not even loaded!'

There is evidence that at about 2.15 a.m., as the forward part of *Titanic*'s starboard boat deck dipped under the water, there was a rush for the last lifeboat, Collapsible A, which Murdoch was preparing for lowering. Several eye witnesses state that they saw an officer shoot one or two passengers at this point and then shoot himself.

The following is an extract from a letter written to his

wife, on April 19th, 1912, by First Class passenger Mr. George Rheims, who escaped in Collapsible A:

> 'As the last lifeboat was leaving I saw an officer kill a man with one gun shot. The man was trying to climb aboard that last lifeboat. Since there was nothing left to do, the officer told us, "Gentlemen, each man for himself, goodbye." He gave us a military salute and shot himself. This was a man!!'

On the same day that he wrote this letter, he gave the same story to the *New York Herald*, who printed it with the following quote from Mr Rheims under the headline 'Officer Kills Man, Ends Own Life':

> 'The majority of men passengers did not attempt to get in the boats. The men assisted the women. But when the boats began to be lowered some men lost their heads. From the lower deck men jumped into crowded boats and others slid down ropes. One officer shot a man who attempted to get into a crowded boat. Immediately afterward the officer said: "Well, goodbye," and killed himself.'

This incident at Collapsible A was also witnessed by Third Class passenger Eugene Daly, who eventually escaped on upturned Collapsible B, as reported by the *Daily Sketch* on Saturday 4th May, 1912:

> '"We afterwards went to the second cabin deck," he

continues, "and the two girls and myself got into a boat. An officer called on me to go back, but I would not stir. They then got hold of me and pulled me out. At the first cabin, when a boat was being lowered, an officer pointed a revolver and said if any man tried to get in he would shoot him on the spot. I saw the officer shoot two men dead because they tried to get into the boat. Afterwards there was another shot, and I saw the officer himself lying on the deck. They told me he shot himself, but I did not see him. I was up to my knees in water at the time. Everyone was rushing around and there were no more boats. I then dived overboard and got in a boat.'"

Third Class passenger Edward Arthur Dorking, who also ended up in Collapsible B with Eugene Daly, told a very similar story to the *Bureau County Republican*, which was printed on 2nd May, 1912:

'An officer stood beside the life-boats as they were being manned and with a pistol in hand, threatened to kill the first man who got into a boat without orders. The rule of "women first" was rigidly enforced. Two stewards hustled into a lifeboat that was being launched. They were commanded to get out by the officers and on refusing to obey the command, were shot down.'

Additional details of Dorking's story had been reported in the April 19th, 1912 edition of *The New York Herald*:

'Almost at the moment I climbed on the raft I could hear pistol shots sounding from the *Titanic*. The sounds of shots had been distinct during all my swim. I don't know how many were fired, but they kept on during all the time I was within hearing distance. I saw an officer, it may have been the captain or it may not, shoot himself before I got away from the ship.'

Another Third Class passenger who also ended up in Collapsible B, Victor Francis Sunderland, confirmed the shooting of a passenger in the April 26th, 1912 edition of the *Cleveland Plain Dealer*, although he did not notice the officer shoot himself afterwards:

'In one boat, partly filled with women and children, sat—I think he was a Russian. An officer told him to get out, but he wouldn't. The officer fired his revolver in the air once or twice and still the man sat there. The officer then shot him and he dropped back in his seat. He was lifted up and dropped overboard.'

But other passengers on this part of the deck at this time do mention an officer's suicide. For example, Carl Jansson, who ended up in Collapsible A with George Reims, as reported in the *Chicago American* on Thurday 25th April, 1912:

'Shortly before the last boat was launched I glanced toward the bridge and saw the chief officer place a revolver in his mouth and shoot himself. His body toppled overboard.'

First Class passenger Mrs. George D. Widener also observed an officer commit suicide from Lifeboat No. 4. Although this was on the port side of the ship, lifeboat No. 4 remained very near and picked several people up from the water; and *Titanic's* list was to port, revealing her decks to boats on this side, and lifeboat No. 4 may have been far enough forward of *Titanic* to see the boat deck on both sides of *Titanic's* bridge. Mrs Widener gave the following account in the *New York Times* of April 20th, 1912:

> 'I went on deck and was put into a life boat. As the boat pulled away from the *Titanic* I saw one of the officers shoot himself in the head, and a few minutes later saw Capt. Smith jump from the bridge into the sea.'

Finally, the following evocative account of seaman Jack Williams, which appeared in the 1912 memorial books, *Titanic and Other Great Sea Disasters*, and *Sinking of the Titanic*, is intriguing, not least because his name is not on the official White Star Line or disaster inquiry crew lists:

> 'The report that it was Murdoch and not Captain Smith who shot himself on the bridge just as the forward section of the *Titanic* sank is true. I still have before me the picture of Murdoch standing on the bridge as the waters surged up about him, placing the pistol to his head and disappearing as the shot that ended his life rang out.'

Although none of this evidence is proof positive that it was Murdoch who shot himself, it does seem that an officer did shoot himself and Murdoch seems the most likely candidate. As *Titanic* experts Bill Wormstedt and Tad Fitch point out in their excellent website *Shots in the dark*, Murdoch was the man directly in charge of the ship in the hours leading up to the collision with the iceberg and he was therefore responsible for the ship and all its passengers during that time. His career at sea was effectively over, even if he survived the disaster, and if 'the' iceberg was not the first to be spotted that night, as brought out in George Behe's *Titanic: Safety, Speed and Sacrifice*, then Murdoch was also responsible for not slowing down, in direct violation of the posted orders from the White Star Line, that 'Time must be sacrificed or any other temporary inconvenience suffered, rather than the lightest risk should be incurred.' He also may not have followed Captain Smith's orders (passed on from Lightoller): 'If in the slightest degree doubtful, let me know at once.'

Certainly, it seems that this is what Dining Room steward Thomas Whitely said he overheard lookouts Fleet and Lee discussing, possibly on the *Carpathia*:

> 'The two men talked freely in his hearing and expressed wonderment that their attempts to get the officer to slow up or take other precautionary methods to avoid the bergs had failed. Mr Whiteley says he carefully marked every word they uttered. "I don't recall the exact words of the men, but I am certain of the sentiment they expressed. They were very indignant. I

was particularly astonished when I heard one of them say:—No wonder Mr Murdoch shot himself.'"

Nevertheless, given that none of this evidence is conclusive, it is worth bearing in mind what Lightoller said about Murdoch's last moments, in the following extract from a letter to his widow:

> 'I was practically the last man, and certainly the last officer, to see Mr. Murdoch. He was then endeavouring to launch the starboard forward collapsible boat. I had already got mine from off the top of our quarters. You will understand when I say that I was working the port side of the ship, and Mr. Murdoch was principally engaged on the starboard side of the ship, filling and launching the boats. Having got my boat down off the top of the house, and there being no time to open it, I left it and ran across to the starboard side, still on top of the quarters. I was then practically looking down on your husband and his men. He was working hard, personally assisting, overhauling the forward boat's fall. At this moment the ship dived, and we were all in the water. Other reports as to the ending are absolutely false. Mr. Murdoch died like a man, doing his duty.'

However, it seems that Lightoller may have dived into the sea just before Murdoch shot himself and thus been unaware of his suicide. It is also possible that Lightoller may have wanted to conceal the suicide, if it occured, from Murdoch's widow.

Second Officer Lightoller and Chief Officer Wilde were both 38 years old, First Officer Murdoch was 39.

83 CAPTAIN SMITH COMMITTED SUICIDE AS THE SHIP WENT DOWN.

No. We have already heard from Steward Brown that Captain Smith was seen walking towards the bridge at the very end, and Harold Bride testified as follows, at the US Inquiry:

> HSB557: (Mr. BRIDE) 'He jumped overboard from the bridge. He jumped overboard from the bridge when we were launching the collapsible lifeboat.'
> HSB558: (Senator SMITH) 'I should judge from what you have said that this was about three or four minutes before the boat sank.'
> Mr. BRIDE: 'Yes. It would be just about five minutes before the boat sank.'

However, Bride could here be mistaking Captain Smith for Lightoller, who we know did exactly this at this time, first swimming towards the crow's nest.

In any event, *Titanic's* barber, August Weikman, said that he had been washed overboard by the same large wave that Colonel Gracie mentions as carrying away his friend James Clinch Smith, and that he had then seen Captain Smith, also apparently washed off by the wave, swimming back towards the ship:

'While this was going on I was on the upper deck assisting the passengers to the boats. I had a life belt on, and when the forward part of the ship listed I was washed overboard by a huge wave. Looking backward, I could see Captain Smith, who had been standing on the bridge, swimming back to the place where he had stood, having been washed off the *Titanic* by the same wave that had washed me from the ship into the water.'

Captain Rostron issued a strong denial of the Smith suicide rumour to the press, saying that some of *Titanic*'s crew had seen him washed off the bridge, reaching the edge of a lifeboat with their assistance, then falling off it again.

This simple account rings true and does tally with others, and combined with Weikman's report, may also explain how the press could have woven into this true story the fiction that he swam with a baby to a lifeboat, and then went back to the ship.

84 MOST TITANIC VICTIMS DROWNED.

No, although about 1,500 passengers and crew died in the sinking. *Titanic* sank in freezing water of between 28 and 32 degrees Fahrenheit, and hypothermia was therefore the cause of death for the majority, who literally froze to death, without any water in their lungs.

Hypothermia sets in more quickly in water, as heat is conducted away from the body 25 times more quickly than in air. In water under 35F, the maximum survival time is usually no more than 45 minutes, with loss of consciousness in less than 15 minutes.

Titanic's lifeboats need not have worried about being swamped if they had returned to pick up swimmers as most of those in the water would therefore have been incapable of swamping a boat or even moving after a very short time. Even mild hypothermia impairs muscular control and dexterity, so those who had been in the water for more than a few minutes would have found it hard to swim towards lifeboats, and it wouldn't have been very long before they became unable even to cry out. Struggling and swimming, which most people would have been doing, or trying to, usually makes cold water hypothermia worse, although exercise is advised for mild hypothermia and was probably what saved most of those sitting on the hull of the upturned Collapsible B, along with the fact that they had managed to get out of the water.

Entering cold water suddenly may cause death more quickly through hyperventilation and inhalation of water or through cardiac arrest from the shock. However, many of those in the water who looked dead may in fact have still been alive, since in some cases of hypothermia, usually when the person's face has come into contact with cold water very suddenly, a dive reflex which is present in all mammals kicks in, allowing the body to preserve oxygen by lowering blood pressure and shutting down all non-essential systems. In these cases, the victim can look dead, but may be revived carefully. This was probably the explanation for the following chilling

testimony from Frank H Morris, who went back to *Titanic*'s
wreck site to look for survivors with Fifth Officer Lowe:

> 5388: 'Is it the case that you could only see three
> people in the water?'
> 'Oh, we saw hundreds in the water, but they were
> not crying for help; they might have been unconscious,
> they might have been dead, we could not say to that.'

In fact, the motto of one hypothermia expert is 'You're not
dead until you're warm and dead', and resuscitation has been
successful after as long as an hour.

A number of deaths may also have been caused by
jumping into the water; if this is done while wearing a
lifejacket and the correct procedure is not followed, severe
injuries can result including a broken neck. This may have
been a contributing factor in the death of some, including
William Hoyt, who was pulled into lifeboat 14 bleeding
from the nose and mouth and died soon after.

Rescue

No. We have already seen that *Titanic*'s final SOS position
41° 44' N, 50° 14' W was about 13 miles west of where
she actually sank and where her wreck was found by Robert
Ballard at 41' 43' N, 49' 56' W. Therefore when *Carpathia*
picked up *Titanic*'s incorrect distress position at 12.35 a.m.,
when she was at about 41'9"N, 49'12"W, the distance
between her and the *Titanic* was incorrectly calculated to
be 58 miles. However, given that *Carpathia* happened to
encounter *Titanic*'s lifeboats while heading straight for this
incorrect position, Captain Rostron naturally assumed that
the distress position he had been given was correct, and
therefore so was the distance.

In fact, it is one of the few pieces of luck *Titanic* enjoyed
that night that her actual wreck site happened to be about on
a straight line between where *Carpathia* was when she picked
up *Titanic*'s distress position at 12.35 p.m. and Boxhall's
incorrect final distress position. Had this not been the case, it
is possible that *Carpathia* could have taken several additional
hours to find *Titanic*'s drifting lifeboats, 13 miles from where

he had been informed the ship went down.

Because *Carpathia* arrived at *Titanic*'s wreck site at about 4 a.m., or three and a half hours after she began her full speed dash, Rostron calculated that *Carpathia* must have averaged 16.5 knots per hour, almost three knots faster than her official top speed of 14 knots. This would have been an extraordinary performance indeed, but we now know that *Titanic*'s wreck site was 13 miles closer to *Carpathia* than her last distress position indicated.

Therefore Capt. Rostron had in fact only travelled about 48 miles to *Titanic*'s wreck site, instead of the 58 miles to Boxhall's incorrect distress position. *Carpathia*'s true average speed was therefore about 13.7 knots. This was nonetheless close to her top speed and therefore a very impressive run, especially considering she had been dodging icebergs since about 3 a.m., when she left the warm waters of the Gulf Stream and entered the freezing Labrador Current, which was bringing large quantities of ice unusually far south that year.

At about 3.15 a.m. Rostron saw a green flare fired by Boxhall in lifeboat No.2. Thinking this was from the sinking *Titanic* herself, Rostron fired one of *Carpathia*'s distress signals in response, and continued to do so every 15 minutes afterwards. Boxhall similarly responded to each of these by continuing to burn his green Roman candles intermittently, until *Carpathia* arrived at Boxhall's boat at 3.55 a.m. Had Boxhall not thought to ship and fire these signals *Carpathia* might well have simply steamed past—or even through— *Titanic*'s lifeboats in the dark, in her dash to reach the incorrect distress position he had been given.

Arthur Rostron certainly pushed *Carpathia* to her limits that night. Passengers remembered the unusual cold, due to the heating in cabins being turned off to enable all available power to reach the engines, and the additional vibration caused by the engines being pushed to their maximum. Nonetheless, *Carpathia* never reached 17.5 knots on that night or any other.

86 CHIEF BAKER CHARLES JOUGHIN SURVIVED FOR SEVERAL HOURS IN THE FREEZING WATER.

Apparently so. *Titanic*'s Chief Baker testified that he survived for several hours in the freezing water, but he wasn't drunk, as is popularly believed. This myth arose because he did admit to having had half a tumbler of liqueur that night.

Despite the inquiry's view that it must have been his alcohol intake that saved him, alcohol wouldn't have helped as it directs blood to the extremities, which gives a feeling of warmth but means that heat is in fact conducted away from the body more quickly. Even the amount he did consume should have made his survival less likely, but his assessment of the amount of time he spent in the freezing water can be verified, at least as far as his own extraordinary account goes:

6077: 'Are you a good swimmer?'
'Yes.'

6078: 'How long do you think you were in the water before you got anything to hold on to?'

'I did not attempt to get anything to hold on to until I reached a collapsible, but that was daylight.'

6079: 'Daylight, was it?'

'I do not know what time it was.'

6080: 'Then you were in the water for a long, long time?'

'I should say over two, hours, Sir.'

6081: 'Were you trying to make progress in the water, to swim, or just keeping where you were?'

'I was just paddling and treading water.'

6082: 'And then daylight broke?'

'Yes.'

6083: 'Did you see any icebergs about you?'

'No, Sir, I could not see anything.'

6084: 'Did it keep calm till daylight, or did the wind rise at all?'

'It was just like a pond.'

6085: 'Then you spoke of a collapsible boat. Tell us shortly about it?'

'Just as it was breaking daylight I saw what I thought was some wreckage, and I started to swim towards it slowly. When I got near enough, I found it was a collapsible not properly upturned but on its side, with an Officer and I should say about twenty or twenty-five men standing on the top of it.'

6098: 'Did you stay near it?'

'I tried to get on it, but I was pushed off it, and I what you call hung around it.'

6099: 'How much later on was it that you were picked up?'

'I eventually got round to the opposite side, and a cook that was on the collapsible recognised me, and held out his hand and held me—a chap named Maynard.'

6100: 'Was he able to pull you out of the water, or was he only just able to help to support you?'

'No.'

6101: 'He gave you a hand, and you kept treading water?'

'No. My lifebelt helped me, and I held on the side of the boat.'

6102: 'You had been wearing a lifebelt?'

'Yes, all the time.'

6103: 'So that your feet would be in the water?'

'Yes, and my legs.'

6104: 'And you supported yourself by your lifebelt. I do not want to be harrowing about it, but was the water very cold?'

'I felt colder in the lifeboat—after I got in the lifeboat.'

6105: 'You were picked up, were you, by a lifeboat later on?'

'We were hanging on to this collapsible, and eventually a lifeboat came in sight.'

6106: 'And they took you aboard?'

'They got within about 50 yards and they sung out that they could only take 10. So I said to this Maynard, "Let go my hand," and I swam to meet it, so that I would be one of the 10.'

6107: 'Did you swim to it, and were you taken in?'

'Yes, I was taken in.'

6108: 'You have said you thought it was about two hours before you saw this collapsible, and then you spent some time with the collapsible. How long do you suppose it was after you got to the collapsible that you were taken into the lifeboat?'

'I should say we were on the collapsible about half-an-hour.'

6109: 'That means that for some two and a half hours you were in the water?'

'Practically, yes.'

We know from Third Officer Pitman that *Titanic* sank at 2.20 a.m.

We also know from several survivors and the rescue ship *Carpathia* that dawn at *Titanic*'s wreck site on Monday 15th April was at 4 a.m. *Titanic* time, with full daylight at 4.30 a.m. Joughin's testimony therefore suggests that he was indeed in the water for around two and a half hours, as he later estimated. Nevertheless, Joughin's testimony is unsupported by any other witness's testimony and it is probable that his recollection of the sequence and timing of the events of his rescue may have been inaccurate.

Indeed, quite how Joughin managed to survive so long, to keep his head and to remember what had happened afterwards, when the upper limit survival time in water of that temperature is approximately 45 minutes, with disorientation and unconsciousness usually occurring within

15 minutes, is anyone's guess. But the fact that his head was not fully wetted would have helped him, trapping pockets of insulating air under his hair. After this if he simply trod water for more than two hours, as he said he did, this also would have helped, as trying to swim tends to make hypothermia worse. He said that he was a good swimmer and, being from Southampton, he would probably have been used to sea swimming. He may also have been wearing a lot of layers and that, combined with a dry head and an apparently unusually hardy constitution, may all have contributed to keep him alive and conscious for far longer than is usually considered possible, and almost certainly for longer than anyone else survived in the water that night.

87 'MOLLY' BROWN TRIED TO MAKE LIFEBOAT NUMBER SIX GO BACK TO PICK UP SURVIVORS, BUT WAS PREVENTED BY QUARTERMASTER ROBERT HICHENS.

Yes. Margaret Brown's own account, told to the *New York Times* on 20th April, 1912, makes no mention of her urging the boat to go back, but the lengthy, two-part account she wrote for the *Newport Herald* states:

> 'When none of the calamities that were predicted by our terrified boatman was experienced, we asked him to return and pick up those in the water. Again we were admonished and told how the frantic drowning

victims would grapple the sides of our boat and capsize us. He not yielding to our entreaties, we pulled away vigorously toward the faintly glimmering light on the horizon.'

Major Arthur Peuchen confirmed that some of the women had wanted to go back, although he did not mention any by name. However, Peuchen and Hichens had a serious disagreement in this boat over Hichen's alleged behavior towards the women:

AGP092: 'While these cries of distress were going on, did anyone in the boat urge the quartermaster to return?'

'Yes; some of the women did. But, as I said before, I had had a row with him, and I said to the women, "It is no use you arguing with that man, at all. It is best not to discuss matters with him." He said it was no use going back there, there was only a lot of stiffs there, later on, which was very unkind, and the women resented it very much. I do not think he was qualified to be a quartermaster.'

Hichens denied that any of the women had wanted to go back or had said anything about it, and that he had said 'stiffs'—but he denied only the use of the word rather than the whole incident. Peuchen's account tallies with what Margaret Brown remembers as far as Hichens is concerned:

'To me there was not one tragic harrowing element near me. We were in a boat, we were safe and we were at work. I was simply fascinated. In a few moments the man in the back of the boat began to complain that we had no chance. There were only three men in the boat. For at least three hours he seemed to break the monotony of it. We stood him patiently, and then after he had told us that we had no chance, told us many times, and after he had explained that we had no food, no water, and no compass I told him to be still or he would go overboard. Then he was quiet. I rowed because I would have frozen to death. I made them all row. It saved their lives.'

However, Peuchen claims that it was he who got the women to row:

AGP137: 'Did any of the women help with the oars?'
'Yes; they did, very pluckily, too. We got the oars. Before this occurred we got a couple of women rowing aft, on the starboard side of our boat, and I got two women to assist on our side; but of course the woman with me got sick with the heavy work, and she had to give it up. But I believe the others kept on rowing quite pluckily for a considerable time.'

Certainly there were women rowing, whether this was instigated by Margaret Brown or Major Peuchen, or both, or one of the other women is not known for certain. However, the main argument that night seems to have been about

Hichens' attitude, rather than the question of returning to pick up survivors. In Hitchen's favour, it should be noted that nearly all Titanic's lifeboats failed to return to pick up survivors, and Hitchen's had been given orders by Second Officer Charles Lightoller to steer lifeboat No. 6 away from *Titanic*, towards a light which could be seen in the distance. Hitchen's did not know that rescue ships were on their way but—as Quartermaster in charge—he would have been better to keep his very understandable fears to himself.

88 MANY MORE PEOPLE WOULD HAVE BEEN SAVED IF MORE LIFEBOATS HAD ATTEMPTED TO RETURN TO PICK UP SURVIVORS FROM THE WATER.

No. By the time *Titanic* sank many of her lifeboats had been pulling slowly away from the ship for about an hour, most because they feared suction, or that a large wave might be caused when she foundered; and some because they were rowing towards the light of the *Californian*, which could be seen on the northern horizon. Many of these boats would have taken about another hour to get back to the *Titanic*'s wreck site, by which time we know from the harrowing testimony of Joseph Scarrott, who went back into the wreckage with Fifth Officer Lowe in lifeboat No. 14 at about 3.30 a.m., nearly everybody in the water was already dead or unconscious:

439: 'And we went away and went among the wreckage. When we got to where the cries were we were amongst hundreds, I should say, of dead bodies floating in lifebelts.'

440: 'Was it dark then?'

'Yes.'

441: 'Still dark?'

'Yes, and the wreckage and bodies seemed to be all hanging in one cluster. When we got up to it we got one man, and we got him in the stern of the boat—a passenger it was, and he died shortly after we got him into the boat. One of the stewards that was in the boat tried means to restore life to the man; he loosed him and worked his limbs about and rubbed him; but it was of no avail at all, because the man never recovered after we got him into the boat. We got two others then as we pushed our way towards the wreckage, and as we got towards the centre we saw one man there. I have since found out he was a storekeeper; he was on top of a staircase; it seemed to be a large piece of wreckage anyhow which had come from some part of the ship. It was wood anyhow. It looked like a staircase. He was kneeling there as if he was praying, and at the same time he was calling for help. When we saw him we were about from here to that wall away from him, and the boats, the wreckage were that thick—and I am sorry to say there were more bodies than there was wreckage— it took us a good half-hour to get that distance to that man to get through the bodies. We could not row the boat; we had to push them out of the way and force our boat up to this man. But we did not get close enough to get him right off—only just within the reach of an oar. We put out an oar on the fore-part of the boat, and he got hold of it, and he managed to hold on, and we got him into the boat. Those three survived. There was one dead in our boat, and that was the passenger, the first one we picked up.'

Even the lifeboats which remained very close to *Titanic* were very slow and hard to manoeuvre, and it was a pitch dark night, so that after her lights had disappeared it was impossible to see exactly where *Titanic* had gone down. Across the flat calm water, it was also impossible to locate exactly where the cries of those in the water were coming from, as we can see from the testimony of John Poingdestre, in charge of lifeboat No. 12. Poingdestre was only 150 yards from where *Titanic* went down and immediately returned to try and help those crying out in the dark:

2990: 'After she sank did you see any people struggling in the water?'
'No.'
2991: 'How far away from the *Titanic* were you?'
'About 150 yards.'
2992: 'After she sank did your boat pull in towards the place where she sank?'
'Yes.'
2993: 'For what purpose?'
'To pick up anybody who was there.'
2994: 'Was there anybody there?'

'I never saw anybody.'

2995: 'Did you see any corpses?'

'No.'

2996: 'You saw nothing?'

'I saw some by daylight.'

2997: 'Did you hear any cries?'

'Yes.'

2998: 'Did not the cries guide you so as to enable you to go to them?'

'Certainly.'

2999: 'Did you go in that direction?'

'I pulled in the direction the cries came from.'

3000: 'Did not you find anybody there?'

'No.'

3001: 'Did you see nobody?'

'Nobody whatever.'

3002: 'Are you sure?'

'Yes.'

3003: 'When you pulled in that direction, did the passengers on board your boat approve of your doing so?'

'Yes.'

3004: 'And you went and searched and found nobody?'

'Yes.'

3005: 'You are sure of that?'

'Yes.'

3013: 'We know what the capacity of the boat is. How long did you remain looking, do you suggest, for the people?'

'About a quarter of an hour.'

3014: 'And you saw nothing?'

'Nothing at all.'

3015: 'Did you see wreckage?'

'Only about a couple of hundred deck chairs.'

3016: 'But you saw no bodies?'

'No bodies whatever.'

3017: 'During that quarter of an hour, while you were looking, how long did the cries continue?'

'All the time that we were looking we heard the cries.'

3018: 'And yet you found nothing?'

'We found nothing at all.'

3019: 'These cries were going on for the whole of the time you were searching?'

'Yes.'

3020: 'What was the nearest do you think that you got to any of these cries?'

'I reckoned about 100 yards.'

3021: 'And then did they cease?'

'Yes.'

3022: 'Can you account for that?'

'I can account for not going to the position where I ought to have been.'

3023: 'Well, will you tell us?'

'There were not enough sailors in my boat, only me and my mate, and we could not get there.'

3024: (The Commissioner) 'Get where?'

'To where the halloes were coming from—the cries.'

About 200 yards was the maximum distance that any survivor claimed to have swum and climbed into a boat, and even then, many of those who got wet did not survive long in the lifeboats, as we learn from the remarkable story of *Titanic's* Lamp Trimmer, Samuel Hemming, who swam to a boat and later helped to pull seven men into it, two of whom died:

> SEH054: 'I went to the bridge and looked over and saw the water climbing upon the bridge. I went and looked over the starboard side, and everything was black. I went over to the port side and saw a boat off the port quarter, and I went along the port side and got up the after boat davits and slid down the fall and swam to the boat and got it.'
>
> SEH055: 'When you say everything looked black, you mean that there were no boats in sight?'
>
> 'Everything was black over the starboard side. I could not see any boats.'
>
> SEH056: 'You swam out to this boat that you saw?'
>
> 'Yes, sir.'
>
> SEH057: 'How far was it from the side of the *Titanic*?'
>
> 'About 200 yards.'
>
> SEH058: 'Did you swim that 200 yards?'
>
> 'Yes.'
>
> SEH059: 'Did you have a lifebelt on?'
>
> 'No, sir.'
>
> SEH060: 'When you reached the boat, what did you find?'
>
> 'I tried to get hold of the grab line on the bows,

and it was too high for me, so I swam along and got hold of one of the grab lines amidships.'

SEH061: 'What did you do then?'

'I pulled my head above the gunwale, and I said, "Give us a hand in, Jack." Foley was in the boat. I saw him standing up in the boat. He said, "Is that you, Sam?" I said, "Yes;" and him and the women and children pulled me in the boat.'

SEH077: 'What was done after you got into the boat?'

'They had been backing her away, to get out of the zone from the ship before the ship sank.'

SEH078: 'You did not return to the ship's side?'

'No, sir.'

SEH079: 'Not at all?'

'No, sir.'

SEH080: 'Or to the place where the ship sank?'

'After the ship had gone we pulled back and picked up seven.'

SEH081: 'Who were they?'

'I am not able to say, sir.'

SEH082: 'Who else?'

'Stewards, firemen, seamen, and one or two men, passengers; I could not say exactly which they were; anyway, I know there were seven altogether.'

SEH095: 'Did they swim to the boat, or did the boat go to the men?'

'Both. They swam toward the boat, and we went back toward them.'

SEH096: 'After you got these seven men in, what did

you do then?'

'We hung around for a bit.'

SEH097: 'Did you see any more men?'

'No, sir.'

SEH098: 'Did you hear any more crying?'

'We heard the cries; yes, sir.'

SEH099: 'Where? In what direction? Toward the *Titanic*?'

'We were moving around, constantly, sir. Sometimes the stern of the boat would be toward the *Titanic*, and sometimes the bow of the boat would be toward the *Titanic*. One moment we would be facing one way, and a few moments later we would be facing another way; first the bow, and then the stern toward the ship.'

SEH100: 'What did you hang around for?'

'We did not know what to do.'

SEH101: 'Did you pick up any more people in the water?'

'Not from the water; no, sir.'

SEH102: 'Did these people that you picked up all live until you reached the *Carpathia*?'

'No, sir.'

SEH103: 'How many died?'

'Two.'

89 SIR COSMO DUFF GORDON OFFERED THOSE IN LIFEBOAT NO. 1 £5 EACH IF THEY WOULD AGREE NOT TO RETURN TO THE SHIP TO PICK UP SURVIVORS.

No. Although Sir Cosmo Duff Gordon did offer the crewmembers in his boat £5 each, it wasn't a bribe to stop them from returning to the wreck site, but a simple gift to help them replace their kit, which they lost when the ship sank; this was also the moment their pay stopped. Unfortunately, this generous action was open to a less generous interpretation after the fact. Sir Cosmo openly admitted to promising the men a present in the boat, a promise which he took pains to carry out:

12584: 'I must ask you about the money. Had you made any promise of a present to the men in the boat?'

'Yes, I did.'

12585: 'Will you tell us about that?'

'I will. If I may, I will tell you what happened.'

12586: 'Yes?'

'There was a man sitting next to me, and of course in the dark I could see nothing of him. I never did see him, and I do not know yet who he is. I suppose it would be some time when they rested on their oars, 20 minutes or half-an-hour after the *Titanic* had sunk, a man said to me, "I suppose you have lost everything," and I said, "Of course." He says, "But you can get some more," and I said, "Yes." "Well," he said, "we have lost all our kit and the company won't give us any more, and what is more our pay stops from tonight. All they will do is to send us back to London." So I said to them: "You fellows need not worry about that; I will give you a fiver each to start a new kit." That is the whole of that £5 note story.'

12591: 'Did you say anything to the Captain of the *Carpathia* of your intention to give that money to the men?'

'Yes; I went to see him one afternoon and told him I had promised the crew of my boat a £5 note each, and he said, "It is quite unnecessary." I laughed and said, "I promised it; so I have got to give it them."'

Sir Cosmo testified that he did not at the time consider it a serious possibility that they could go back to rescue those in the water, but that he certainly never said that they should not go back.

Fireman Charles Hendrickson, on the other hand, claimed that the boat had failed to go back only because the Duff Gordons had prevented it, saying it would be too dangerous and that they would be swamped. Hendrickson also said that Sir Cosmo Duff Gordon did give the crew members in the lifeboat £5 on the *Carpathia*, having promised 'a little present' shortly before they were rescued. However, Hendrickson also testified that he had no expectation of the £5 when the discussion about going back took place, and that at this point it hadn't been mentioned.

Samuel Collins, a fireman in the same boat, had a different version of events which contradicted Hendrickson and supported Sir Cosmo's testimony. According to Collins, the Duff Gordons had not said anything about swamping, nor had any other passenger. There was some discussion about the dangers of suction from the sinking ship, but this was mainly between the crew. Collins also said he had heard nothing about money until he was carrying someone's coat up the ladder to the *Carpathia* and was asked by the coat's owner (Sir Cosmo Duff Gordon, although Collins didn't know this at the time) to get the names of the crew of the boat, a task which Hendrickson subsequently took over. The envelope with the money was a 'complete surprise' according to Collins, who apparently had no idea of what it was beforehand, or any expectation of receiving something.

Regardless of the details on this point, the evidence clearly suggests that Sir Cosmo's action was no more than a generous gesture; and that attempting to row back to find the screaming throng in the dark simply did not occur to him as a serious possibility.

90 THE BARKING OF A NEWFOUNDLAND DOG ALERTED CARPATHIA TO TITANIC'S LIFEBOATS.

No. The story of 'Rigel the wonder dog' is almost certainly— in nearly every sense of the phrase—a shaggy dog story. It seems to have originated in press reports from 1912, probably started by Jonas Briggs, who falsely claimed to have been a crewmember aboard the *Carpathia*. According to his account, Rigel was a big black Newfoundland dog who belonged to First Officer Murdoch. The story goes that the dog had swum in the icy water, near lifeboat No. 4, for three hours, probably looking for his master, and alerted the *Carpathia's* crew by barking. The lifeboat might not have been rescued if not for the sharp barking of Rigel, as Captain Rostron saw the boat on the starboard side of the bridge thanks to his sharp barking and ordered the engines stopped. Care was taken to get Rigel on board, but he appeared little affected by his long trip through the ice-cold water. He stood by the rail and barked until Captain Rostron called Briggs and had him take the dog below. Jonas Briggs said he then kept the dog.

The dog is not mentioned by Fourth Officer Boxhall in lifeboat No. 2—the first boat to be picked up—nor any of the survivors in lifeboat No. 4, so the Rigel story is almost certainly a fabrication. However, a few days after the sinking the German ship *Bremen* passed near *Titanic's* wreck site and saw a field of bodies, including a shaggy dog, and debris floating in the water. Passenger Johanna Stunke described the awful scene as follows:

'We passed within a hundred feet of the southernmost drift of the wreckage, and looking down over the rail we distinctly saw a number of bodies so clearly that we could make out what they were wearing and whether they were men or women.

'We saw one woman in her night dress, with a baby clasped closely to her breast. Several women passengers screamed and left the rail in a fainting condition. There was another woman, fully dressed, with her arms tight around the body of a shaggy dog.'

It's been suggested that this was Ann Isham, who allegedly brought a Great Dane on board and refused to leave it, but there's no evidence to support this. However, several passengers did bring dogs on board, including two Pomeranians, a Pekinese called Sun Yat-Sen belonging to Henry Sleeper Harper which was rescued in lifeboat No. 3 with its owner, two French bulldogs and an Airedale terrier named Kitty belonging to the Astors, which did not survive. Master William Carter vividly remembered having to leave his own Airedale behind when he got into boat No. 4, Col. Astor promising to look after the dog for him.

Claims that there was a pack of hunting hounds on board were, however, untrue. First Class passenger Clarence Moore, who died in the sinking, had been to England to buy fifty pairs of hounds for his hunt, but he did not take them on board with him.

91 OPERATORS ON THE CARPATHIA WITHHELD INFORMATION ABOUT TITANIC'S SINKING IN ORDER TO SELL THEIR STORY TO THE PAPERS.

No. Both Bride and Cottam, the *Carpathia's* wireless operator, admitted that they did not provide information about the sinking to everyone who asked. They also admitted that they had been asked by the Marconi Company to save their story and sell it to the newspapers. However, Captain Rostron of the *Carpathia* had ordered them to prioritise survivor messages and official business, including White Star Line and Cunard messages, and to ignore everything else. Bride and Cottam insisted that their actions arose from the orders of Captain Rostron, who was motivated only by expediency; and that these overrode the orders from their employer.

The volume of messages was so great that Cottam sent over 500 messages from survivors and was awake for most of the time between the *Carpathia* picking up the *Titanic's* distress signal and docking in New York several days later. At one point Cottam fell asleep over his set and had to be relieved by Bride, the *Titanic's* injured wireless operator.

President Taft, whose military aide, Major Archibald Butt, was a passenger on *Titanic*, sent the USS *Chester* out to meet the *Carpathia* to try and get news of Major Butt (who had been lost in the sinking). It caused an uproar in America that the *Chester's* requests for information were not complied with fully, but this was purely the result of the instructions Bride and Cottam had received from Captain Rostron. The *Chester* had requested a list of *Titanic* passengers and crew aboard *Carpathia*, but Captain Rostron told Cottam to respond with a list of Third Class passengers only as Cottam had already sent all the other names ashore. Neither Cottam nor Rostron was aware that the message was actually from President Taft, as it was signed by Commander Decker of the *Chester*. Several hours later, Bride transmitted the Third Class passenger names, which he said took a long time due to repeated misunderstandings on the part of the *Chester's* operator; this was probably due to differences in the wireless systems used by each ship.

However, the rumour of withholding information for personal gain arose because it became known that the following messages were sent to the *Carpathia* by the Marconi Company and received by Bride:

8.12 P.M.

SEAGATE TO CARPATHIA:
Say, old man. Marconi Co. taking good care of you. Keep your mouth shut and hold your story; It is fixed for you so you will get big money. Now, please do your best to clear.

8:30 P.M.

To Marconi officer, Carpathia and Titanic:
Arranged for your exclusive story for dollars in four figures. Mr. Marconi agreeing. Say nothing until you see me. Where are you now?

J. M. SAMMIS, Opr. C.

Both Marconi and Sammis thought that it was not unreasonable that the operators should make some money out of their story, just as Jack Binns, the wireless operator on the RMS *Republic* who had sent the first CQD by wireless from a ship, had done a few years earlier, and Sammis admitted sending a message to the *Carpathia*, asking Cottam and Bride to come to the Strand Hotel to meet a reporter from the *New York Times*.

Bride and Cottam both remembered that the earlier messages, asking them to 'keep their mouth shut', had been received, but were adamant that this had not influenced them, and that they had, as ordered by the captain, simply prioritised official messages and passenger traffic. Bride did subsequently sell his story to a *New York Times* reporter who came on board *Carpathia* along with Mr Marconi and Mr Sammis, for $500. Cottam left the ship as soon as she docked, but later received $750 from the *New York Times* for his story.

Statistics

92 A HIGHER PERCENTAGE OF IRISH PEOPLE DIED ON THE TITANIC THAN ANY OTHER NATIONALITY.

No. The number of Irish passengers on the *Titanic* was in fact relatively low, although several films have given the impression that the Irish dominated Third Class. In fact, even if it is assumed that all those embarking at Queenstown (now Cobh) were Irish, there were only 113 Irish passengers in Third Class, of whom 40 were saved, or 35.4%, while of 183 non-Irish British passengers, only 38 were saved, or 20.8%. Only 100 non-British Third Class passengers were saved out of 410, or 24.4%, making Irish people more likely to survive the sinking of the *Titanic* than any other ethnic group. However, of the five children under the age of 12 who embarked at Queenstown, none survived the sinking.

93A A HIGHER PERCENTAGE OF THIRD CLASS MEN DIED THAN SECOND CLASS MEN.

No. Approximately twice as many Third Class men were saved than Second Class men, as a percentage of their classes.

Only 14 of 175 adult Second Class men survived, or 8%; compared with either 75 of 462 or 55 of 454 Third Class men, depending on which statistics in the British Enquiry have been correctly printed. Either way, this is a total of 16 % or 12% of Third Class men saved, both of which are significantly higher than the only 8% of Second Class men saved.

93B MORE FIRST CLASS MEN WERE SAVED THAN THIRD CLASS MEN.

No. 60 men survived from Third Class and only 58 survived from First Class. However, this is unsurprising given that there were 450 men in Third Class and only 176 men in First Class. The actual survival rate is therefore considerably higher for First Class men, at 33%, than Third Class men, only 13% of whom survived.

93C A HIGHER PERCENTAGE OF TITANIC'S MALE PASSENGERS WERE SAVED THAN CREW.

No. 22% of *Titanic*'s crew were saved, as opposed to only 16% of *Titanic*'s male passengers. This was because several crew members were required to be in each lifeboat, to handle steering and rowing, etc. and all the deck and engine room crew were men. This resulted in more crew being allowed to get into lifeboats than male passengers, who had to wait under the rule of women and children first. Crew members saved included several officers, such as Third Officer Pitman, who was told by First Officer Murdoch to go with lifeboat No. 5, after helping to load it; and *Titanic's* navigating officer, Fourth Officer Boxhall, who was ordered to take charge of lifeboat No. 2 by Captain Smith. Major Peuchen, a passenger who was also an experienced yachtsman, also survived in this way, when Lightoller allowed him to go as crew in lifeboat number six, to avoid it going away undermanned.

93D MORE WOMEN WERE SAVED FROM THE TITANIC THAN MEN.

No, in total, 338 men were saved from the *Titanic* and only 316 women. Again, this was a function of the fact that *Titanic's* crew included 862 men, but only 23 women. *Titanic* therefore carried a total of 1,667 male passengers and crew, as against only 425 women passengers and crew. In other words, only about 25% of people on *Titanic* were women.

Aftermath

94 BODIES OF FIRST AND SECOND CLASS PASSENGERS WERE
TAKEN TO HALIFAX FOR BURIAL, BUT THIRD CLASS PASSENGERS
WERE BURIED AT SEA.

No. The only bodies buried at sea were those which couldn't be
identified because they were recovered from the sea in such a
poor state. The *Mackay-Bennett*, which was the first ship sent
out to recover the bodies, took—in addition to embalming
fluid and ice—12 tons of grate iron for committing bodies
to the deep. Of 306 bodies recovered by the *Mackay-Bennett*,
116 were buried at sea; 19 more were found by other vessels
of which three were buried at sea. Nevertheless, when news
of the *Mackay-Bennett's* practice reached shore, there was
an outcry from the families of victims and thereafter no
recovered bodies were buried at sea. Those which were buried
at sea, however, had been given a proper burial service, and
the *Mackay-Bennett's* captain, who would have preferred this
to a burial on land for himself, thought it appropriate at least
for the crew, who had 'lived by the sea'.

There was, however, a class distinction in the way the
bodies were stored on the ship. First Class were embalmed
and kept in coffins, with Second and Third Class simply being
sewn into canvas bags. The bodies of *Titanic's* crew were just

stowed in the hold, in ice. However, the classification was generally done by the clothing and effects found with the bodies, and since a number of people were wearing items of clothing which had been borrowed or even taken from others on the ship, there were several misidentifications.

The burials at sea were arranged partly due to the shortage of embalming fluid; regulations stated that bodies could not be brought ashore unembalmed. However, the *Halifax Evening Mail* of April 30th says that the dead crew were brought from the *Mackay-Bennett* unembalmed and in a horrible state, due presumably to them being kept in ice. Perhaps, due to the large numbers of bodies, this regulation had been waived, as some bodies were certainly embalmed in the Mayflower Curling Rink in Halifax. Those bodies which could not be identified were buried in graves marked with numbers.

95 ONE OF TITANIC'S LIFEBOATS WAS FOUND DRIFTING IN THE ATLANTIC A MONTH AFTER THE SINKING WITH THE BODIES OF THREE VICTIMS STILL IN IT.

Yes. This was collapsible A, found by the *Oceanic* on 13th May, 1912, several hundred miles south-east of *Titanic*'s wreck site. One of the bodies was that of First Class passenger Thomson Beattie; the other two were never identified, although it is possible that one was that of Third Class passenger Arthur Keefe. Sir Shane Leslie, a passenger on board the *Oceanic*, described the scene:

'The sea was calm at noon when the watch called out that something could be seen floating ahead. The ship slowed down and it was apparent that the object was an open ship's lifeboat floating in mid Atlantic. What was horrifying is that it contained three prostrate figures. Orders from the bridge dispatched a lifeboat with an officer and a medical officer. What followed was ghastly. Two sailors could be seen, their hair bleached by exposure to sun and salt, and a third figure, wearing evening dress, flat on the benches. All three were dead and the bodies had been tossing on the Atlantic swell under the open sky ever since it had seen the greatest of ocean liners sink. The three bodies were sewn into canvas bags with a steel bar at the end of each. Then one after the other the bodies were draped in the Union Jack, the burial service was read, and they splashed into the sea.'

Fifth Officer Lowe had left these bodies in Collapsible A after transferring all those who were still alive into his own boat, No. 14. At the US enquiry, he said that he had left the bodies of the three men only after he was absolutely sure that they were dead, as he was concentrating on saving only those who were still alive:

HGL686: (Senator SMITH) 'What became of the other three that you left on it?'
(Mr. LOWE): 'As to the three people that I left on her—of course, I may have been a bit hard hearted, I can not say—but I thought to myself, "I am not here

to worry about bodies; I am here for life, to save life, and not to bother about bodies," and I left them.'

96 THE TITANIC AND HER CARGO WERE RE-INSURED IMMEDIATELY AFTER THE DISASTER.

No. In fact, *Titanic* was only insured by third parties for two thirds of her build cost—the balance being carried by her ultimate owners, the International Mercantile Marine Co.—and her cargo was not insured at all. Senator Smith went into the matter of *Titanic*'s possible re-insurance in considerable detail at the US enquiry:

PAF344: 'You say the *Titanic* cost, complete, one million and a half pounds, in round numbers. What was she insured for?'

'She was insured for, in round numbers, £1,000,000, the balance being carried by the I. M. M. Co., under our own underwriting scheme.

'Adding to that, I would like to say that I do not believe there is any company crossing the Atlantic that carries such a large proportion of its own insurance as the subsidiary companies of the International Mercantile Marine Co.'

PAF668: 'Between the time that you received this information from Montreal and the time you made public the information which you received from

Montreal, did your company reinsure the *Titanic* or its cargo anywhere?'

'Absolutely, no.'

PAF669: 'Did you make any endeavour to reinsure with the Lloyd's in England?'

'None whatever.'

PAF670: 'Are you speaking now for all the officers of your company, here and abroad?'

'I say this, that our insurance is handled in our New York office, and I am sure that nobody would have taken any action regarding it, or have done anything in connection with it, for account of our company or anybody connected with the company in any way, without first having taken it up with me.

'I might say that through the entire day we told the newspaper representatives, who were there all the time—we got our first information from the newspapers, and we told the newspapers all the time— that our only authentic information was coming from Capt. Haddock [of the *Olympic*] and we were giving them that.'

PAF677: 'If your officials in Liverpool or London, or any place else, had reinsured your cargo would you have known it?'

'I would certainly have had the advice. But there was nobody in England who was in any way connected with the insurance department and nobody there who would have taken any action in connection with insurance matters. I might say we carry no insurance on the cargo, Senator.'

PAF678: 'None at all?'

'We only insure the freight money; the insurance is not on the cargo itself, but on the freight money.'

PAF679: 'This ship was insured for $4,000,000?'

'This ship was insured with outside underwriters for $5,000,000, in round figures. It was, in pounds, about a million pounds. The company carried the remainder, up to about £600,000—between £500,000 and £600,000. That is, our insurance fund carried the remainder.'

97 THE SHIP THAT SANK WAS ACTUALLY THE PREVIOUSLY DAMAGED OLYMPIC IN AN INSURANCE SCAM THAT WENT WRONG.

No. But it has nevertheless been suggested by one author that *Olympic*'s collision with the Navy cruiser HMS *Hawke* and subsequent problems with her propeller blades meant that it had become cheaper to 'lose' her and claim the insurance. Supposedly, the *Baltic* was to have been standing by to pick up passengers from the sinking *Olympic*, which had been secretly swapped for the *Titanic*, but the plan went catastrophically wrong, resulting in 1,500 deaths.

However, even if this 'switch' could have been accomplished—which would have been difficult given the large numbers of people who would have had to be involved and kept absolutely quiet—any deliberate sinking would have been disastrous for the White Star Line's reputation for building safe ships and therefore for its finances. In addition, we have already seen that *Olympic* and *Titanic* were each insured for considerably less than their build costs, with a large part of their insurance being underwritten by White Star Line's parent company, the International Mercantile Marine Company; this would make any corporate claim from White Star partly an 'own goal' for the Group.

Finally, concrete evidence backs up the commonsense argument: the *Titanic*'s hull number, 401 (*Olympic*'s was 400), is the only one which has ever been found on *Titanic*'s wreck.

98 ISMAY DEVELOPED A LIFELONG OPIATE ADDICTION AFTER THE SINKING AND WITHDREW FROM SOCIETY.

No, but he did withdraw from society to a large extent. In his book, *A Night To Remember*, Walter Lord describes Ismay as being in shock and drugged on opiates until the *Carpathia* reached New York, and afterwards remaining a 'virtual recluse' in Ireland. The wireless traffic does show that Ismay was given a sedative by *Carpathia*'s doctor after coming aboard, in the following telegram from Captain Rostron of the rescue ship *Carpathia* to Captain Haddock of the *Olympic*, sent at around 7.30 a.m. on the morning of the 15th April, 1912:

'Carpathia'
'CAPTAIN Olympic:'
Bruce Ismay is under opiate.
ROSTRON.

As we have seen, Ismay was offered coffee when he arrived aboard the *Carpathia*, which he refused saying only: 'I wish you would get me somewhere where I can be quiet' and one can well imagine that he was keen to avoid meeting the many women on *Carpathia*'s decks who had lost their husbands, when he had got into a lifeboat—particularly those in First Class to whom he had bragged about *Titanic*'s speed and the likelihood of an early arrival in New York, despite the ice conditions.

He was nevertheless sufficiently in control of himself to send wireless messages to New York, including a message to the White Star Line informing them of what had happened. As we have seen, this message was prepared on the morning of the 15th April, although it was not received in New York until the 17th. Ismay also sent several other wireless messages whilst aboard the *Carpathia*, including one stating that the White Star Line's *Cedric* should be held back in New York to wait for *Titanic*'s surviving crew to arrive aboard the *Carpathia*, so they could be kept together and be returned immediately to England. He also appeared fit and well at 10.30 a.m. the morning after the *Carpathia* arrived in New York, when he appeared before Senator Smith as the first witness at the US Inquiry into the *Titanic* disaster.

Ismay was tall, fit and only 52 years old when *Titanic* sank, and he was at that time already Chairman of the

International Mercantile Marine Company, which owned a larger percentage of all transatlantic shipping than any other company, by a long way. As a young man at Harrow, Ismay was a renowned athlete and sportsman and there is no evidence of his using drugs habitually, at any time in his life.

As for withdrawing from public life, there is some truth in this rumour. Ismay retired as a director of the White Star Line in 1913, although an article in the London *Times* in January 1913 announcing his retirement was at pains to explain that he had expressed his wish to retire two months before the *Titanic* disaster in February of 1912, ceding his post to Harold Sanderson; the retirement was to be effective from June 1913. Ismay still retained several other company directorships after the sinking, although in 1913 he purchased a large house in a very secluded spot in County Galway, on the west coast of Ireland. The house is completely surrounded by walls eight feet high and is situated near quiet salmon fishing pools, where Ismay liked to relax.

His obituary in the *Times* mentions his generosity towards the 'needy inhabitants' of County Galway, and he kept up his habit of charitable donations, giving £11,000 to a fund for the widows of lost seamen, and in 1919 giving £25,000 to a fund which aimed to recognise the contributions of merchant seamen during the war. He also inaugurated the cadet ship *Mersey*, for the training of merchant navy officers, and oversaw the rebuilding of his house in Ireland after it was burnt down by the IRA in 1925. However, it seems that by the mid 1920s he had retired from active life and begun to spend most of his time in Ireland, later returning to England, where he died on October 17th, 1937, of a stroke arising from complications with diabetes; he was buried in Putney Vale cemetery

Ismay was understandably affected by the publicity which accompanied the *Titanic*'s sinking and by the accusations of cowardice and recklessness levelled against him. His wife was said to have remarked 'That ship ruined our lives', and the couple disliked any mention of the *Titanic*.

In his book *The Night Lives On*, Walter Lord described Ismay's post-*Titanic* life as follows:

'After the *Titanic* Ismay never participated in public functions. He never attended Mrs Ismay's frequent bridge parties and dances. He never travelled to America again. He amused himself sitting on a park bench, chatting anonymously with down-and-outers. He liked to watch passing parades, looking at them alone and lost in the crowd.'

99 THE BRITISH INQUIRY INTO THE SINKING WAS A WHITEWASH.

Yes, much of the horrific loss of life which occurred in the *Titanic* disaster could have been prevented if the British Board of Trade had not allowed itself to be lulled into a false sense of security by the ship owners who advised it, through the Merchant Shipping Advisory Committee. Much of the blame therefore lay at the feet of the Board of Trade; and yet it was this very same body which commissioned the Inquiry into the *Titanic* disaster.

Lightoller frankly admitted that the British Inquiry was a whitewash, in the following candid and poignant passage in his 1935 memoir, *Titanic and other Ships*:

'In Washington it was of little consequence, but in London it was very necessary to keep one's hand on the whitewash brush. Sharp questions that needed careful answers if one was to avoid a pitfall... How hard [the lawyers] tried to prove there were not enough seamen to launch and man the boats..., and quite truly. But it was inadvisable to admit it then and there, hence the hard fought legal duals between us.

'A washing of dirty linen would help no one. The B.O.T. had passed that ship as in all respects fit for sea in every sense of the word. Now the B.O.T was holding an inquiry in to the loss of that ship—hence the whitewash brush. Personally, I had no desire that blame should be attributed either to the B.O.T. or the White Star Line, though in all conscience it was a difficult task...when one had known, full well, and for many years, the ever-present possibility of just such a disaster. I think in the end the B.O.T. and the White Star Line won.

'...the utter inadequacy of the life-saving equipment then prevailing...has since been wholly, frankly, and fully admitted by the stringent rules now governing British ships, "Going Foreign".

'No longer is the Boat-Deck almost wholly set aside as a recreation ground for passengers, with the smallest number of boats relegated to the least possible space.

'In fact, the pendulum has swing to the other extreme and the margin of safety reached the ridiculous.

'I know when it was all over I felt more like a legal doormat than a Mail Boat Officer.

'Still, just that word of thanks which was lacking, which when the *Titanic* Enquiry was all over would have been very much appreciated. Yet, when after 20 years of service I came to bury my anchor, and awaited their pleasure at headquarters, for the last time, there was a brief, "Oh, you are leaving us, are you? Well, Good-bye."

'A curious people!'

Certainly, Lightoller gave a polished performance on the stand, which even impressed Lord Mersey with its cleverness, if not its complete honesty:

The Commissioner: 'I suppose I am obliged to accept Lightoller's statement about that conversation?' [Author's note: this refers to Lightoller's conversation on *Titanic*'s bridge with Captain Smith about the weather conditions that night.]
The Attorney-General: 'Well, I do not know.'
The Commissioner: 'I do not like these precise memories; I doubt their existence. However, there it is.'

The Attorney-General: 'There it is, and we have to deal with it on the evidence. The reason why I am dealing with Lightoller's evidence is because Lightoller is the only person who makes this excuse.' [Author's note: this excuse was the calm sea and moonless night, making icebergs hard to detect.]

The Commissioner: 'Yes, and it sounds to me so like an excuse.'

The Attorney-General: 'It is right to say this is it not— your Lordship is a better judge than I am from every point of view, and I was not here during the whole of the time when Lightoller was giving his evidence— that he did give it very well.'

The Commissioner: 'It is to be remembered that he told exactly or practically the same story in America.'

The Attorney-General: 'Yes, from the first. I think it is right to say with regard to Lightoller, is it not, that he gave his evidence very well.'

The Commissioner: 'He gave it remarkably well.'

The Attorney-General: 'Too well your Lordship thinks?'

The Commissioner: 'Well, remarkably well.'

The structural problems with the British Inquiry were even raised with Lord Mersey himself, in the following exchange, where he assures Mr Edwards, Council for the Dockers' Union, of his own impartiality:

Mr. Edwards: 'With this one consideration, My Lord. It is said by the Attorney-General that there is no reason why there should be any departure from the ordinary practice in relation to these Enquiries; but there is this distinction between this Enquiry and others, which I would suggest to your Lordship, and that is this, that not only is there a question here of the conduct of the owners of the *Titanic*, but there is also a question here as to the conduct of the Marine Department of the Board of Trade. Now, the learned Attorney-General is here, of course, in a dual capacity. He represents the Board of Trade, as he represents those who are responsible for formulating the charges. Now, I do suggest if he does not begin the address to your Lordship on the general question, he at least ought to be in the position of addressing your Lordship on behalf of the Board of Trade, so that those of us who stand in a position somewhat adverse to the conduct of the Marine Department of the Board of Trade should have an opportunity of replying to whatever defense is set up.'

The Commissioner: 'I do not think I should allow that, Mr. Edwards. I regard you and Mr. Scanlan and various others—but you two mainly—as the accusers of the Board of Trade, and I shall expect you to put forward your case against the Board of Trade, and to explain to me what it is you allege against the conduct of the Board of Trade, and the Attorney-General will deal with that, not in the spirit of an advocate for the Board of Trade, but as a man trying to assist me, and nothing else; and I think, Myself, if I may say so, that he has taken that course, so far, quite impartially.'

Nonetheless, many representatives of the Board of Trade were questioned closely during the British Inquiry and several criticisms of it were made, including in the following impassioned speech by Mr Harbinson, representing Third Class passengers:

'…The learned Attorney-General has a big task, I think before him when he comes to vindicate the Board of Trade because, if I may say so, I think to seek to defend the Board of Trade is like defending the indefensible. Its position is serious. It wakes up in 1894, and it makes Rules with reference to vessels up to 10,000 tons, and then, my Lord, it goes to sleep and it does nothing. There is nothing done, no steps taken to extend the scale, although vessels are built between 1894 and 1910 which leap up in tonnage from 10,000 to between 40,000 and 50,000 tons… I wish to say that the Board of Trade has got many eyes and many ears, but it does not seem to have any brains. And although it gets information from all sides it does not seem to be able to digest it, to assimilate it, or to apply it; and if, as the result of this awful tragedy the Board of Trade could be modernised, and made, as it were, the reflex of the living, throbbing and palpitating life of this country, then I should think, at all events, appalling, world-wide as this calamity has been, my Lord, it will have borne some fruit.'

Despite its obvious structural failings, the British Inquiry did genuinely try and get at a number of the facts, and it came to broadly the same conclusions as the American Enquiry, which cannot be said to have been similarly compromised. Indeed, these Inquiries have given us a record of more than 2,000 pages of testimony, much of it from eye witnesses, without which we would know a great deal less about the *Titanic*; and Lord Mersey did make some useful recommendations, including lifeboats for all, 24-hour radio watch, more frequent boat drills and improved watertight integrity standards for ships.

100 RMS TITANIC INC. NOW OWNS THE WRECK.

No. RMS *Titanic* Inc. does have 'salvor-in-possession' rights as a descendant of *Titanic* Ventures, which was the first to bring up objects from the wreck and was therefore automatically awarded those rights, but under maritime law the salvor-in-possession is an agent of the court, which ultimately retains control over the wreck. The salvor-in-possession must maintain a periodic physical presence in order to keep their status, and is permitted to remove objects from the debris field, including pieces of the ship which have fallen away from the main structure, but not to remove anything from the main wreck.

The Fourth Circuit Court of Appeals in Virginia ruled in 2002 that RMST does not have legal title to the artefacts which they have brought up as the salvor-in-possession and cannot therefore sell them to maintain their economic position, although in some cases title may be granted to a salvor if sale of the artefacts will not recoup the cost of salvage.

RMS *Titanic* Inc.'s approach has been criticised by many who consider that they are exploiting the wreck for commercial gain, although the company has raised valid arguments in favour of bringing up artefacts from the wreck, pointing out that they have valuable educational and cultural benefit, and that the wreck is deteriorating rapidly and will not be there forever. It has been suggested that George Tulloch, RMST's former president, was dismissed from the company because he had failed to bring in enough profit from the venture.

Dr Robert Ballard, who found the wreck and waived his salvor-in-possession rights by leaving it untouched, is among those who think that it should be designated a gravesite and a monument to victims of the disaster.

In 1986 this approach gained some official support with the passing of the RMS *Titanic* Maritime Memorial Act in the US House of Representatives, which aims to protect the wreck site from unwarranted looting, and to gain support for having the wreck declared a maritime memorial which cannot be used for profit.

IOI THE WRECK OF THE TITANIC MAY ONE DAY BE RAISED.

Probably not. The wreck of the *Titanic* really is a wreck, as Dr Robert Ballard discovered at 1.05 a.m. on 1st September, 1985. *Titanic* is lying in pitch darkness under 12,460 feet of water, which generates a pressure of 6,000 lbs per square inch on the seabed. She is torn into two huge pieces 1,970 feet apart, each with its own debris field over 2,000 feet long, containing much of *Titanic*'s mid-section and contents. There is therefore no possibility of her eventual triumphant arrival into New York, such as that which was depicted in the 1980 film, *Raise The Titanic*.

Given *Titanic*'s poor condition and her extreme depth, current technology is nowhere near advanced enough to be able to raise her on anything like a commercial basis. The discovery of the *Titanic* was estimated to cost a total of $15 million dollars in 1985, given the equipment which was used. The expedition was funded by the combined resources of the US Navy, the French government and the National Geographic Society. If *Titanic* ever did get raised, it would be for the love of her, not the money. But as we wait for new technologies to develop which would make this a practical possibility, *Titanic* is rusting away on the seabed. The wreck is deteriorating relatively rapidly due to the activity of marine organisms which are actually eating the steel and leaving it streaming down the sides of the ship in deposits which Ballard dubbed 'rusticles', because they look like icicles made of rust.

The exploration of *Titanic* is also playing a part in her deterioration, with damage being caused by activities such as submersibles landing on her deck. However, RMS *Titanic* Inc. raised a 17-ton portion of the hull in 1998 and it's likely that some other very large pieces may yet be raised, including a recently discovered, intact, but detached, complete section of *Titanic*'s double bottom. These pieces may yet tell us a lot about *Titanic*'s break-up, and the wreck may one day reveal more details about the exact nature of her collision.

Perhaps most valuably of all, what remains of her wreck will always serve as a tangible reminder of the price we pay for overconfidence.

Acknowledgements

I would like to thank my co-author Eloise Aston for all her hard work, research and enthusiasm and my publisher Simon Petherick at Beautiful Books, without whom this book would never have existed; but most of all I would like to thank The Titanic Historical Society and all the Titanic experts on whom my research has been based, many of whom have become friends of mine. Particularly George Behe, Sam Halpern and Bruce Beveridge, who assisted greatly in getting this text into reasonable shape. Finally, I would like to thank my wife and children for allowing me the time to read and annotate all of the American and British Inquiries into the disaster and to pull this text together.

Bibliography

BALLARD, Robert D. *The discovery of the Titanic.* London: Hodder and Stoughton, 1987.

BEESLEY, Lawrence. *The loss of the SS. Titanic: its story and its lessons.* Cambridge, Massachusetts: William Heinemann, 1912.

BEHE, George. *Titanic: Safety, Speed and Sacrifice.* Polo, Illinois: Transportation Trails, 1997.

BISSET, James, Sir. *Tramps and ladies: my early years with steamers.* Wellingborough: Stephens, 1988.

BRITISH *TITANIC* INQUIRY. The Journal of commerce report of the *Titanic* inquiry: reprinted from *The Journal of Commerce.* London, Liverpool: Journal of Commerce, 1912.

CHIRNSIDE, Mark. *RMS Olympic: Titanic's sister.* Stroud: Tempus, 2005.

GRACIE, Archibald. *The truth about the Titanic.* New York: M. Kennerley, 1913.

JESSOP, Violet. *Titanic Survivor.* Stroud: Sutton Publishing Ltd, 1998.

LIGHTOLLER, C. H. *Titanic and other ships.* London: I. Nicholson & Watson, 1935.

LORD, Walter. *A Night To Remember.* London: Longmans, Green, 1956.

LORD, Walter. *The Night Lives On.* New York: William Morrow & Co, 1986.

READE, Leslie. *The ship that stood still: the Californian and her mysterious role in the Titanic disaster.* Sparkford: Patrick Stephens, 1993.

ROSTRON, Arthur Henry, Sir. *Home From The Sea.* London: Cassell & Co., 1931.

THAYER, John B., *The Sinking of the S. S. Titanic April 14-15, 1912,* Indian Orchard, Massachusetts: 7 C's Press, 1974.

THE US TITANIC INQUIRY. US Senate, 1912.

Webliography

Encyclopedia Titanica: http://www.encyclopedia-titanica. org.

George Behe's Titanic Tidbits: http://home.comcast. net/~georgebehe/titanic/index.html.

Mark Chirnside: www.markchirnside.co.uk.

Titanicology (Halpern, Sam): www.titanicology.com.

Titanic inquiry poject: www.titanicinquiry.org.

Wormstedt, *Shots In The Dark* (Wormstedt, Bill et al.): http://wormstedt.com.